WHO AM I?

WHO AM I?

HOW TO BE A CHRISTIAN WOMAN WHEN YOU JUST CAN'T SEEM TO FIGURE IT OUT...

JAIME LEE

XULON PRESS

Xulon Press
2301 Lucien Way #415
Maitland, FL 32751
407.339.4217
www.xulonpress.com

Paperback ISBN-13: 978-1-66286-532-9
Ebook ISBN-13: 978-1-66286-533-6

Contents

Introduction

I was standing in the bathroom looking at myself in the mirror, and I began to critique God's design as I had done time and time again. He created me in His image and crafted me into who I am, He knitted me in my mother's womb (Psalms 139:13-16 NLT), and He knew every hair He would place on my head (Luke 12:7 NLT). Yet here I am again, picking myself a part with words like;

"Your lips are uneven."

"You're too young for so many wrinkles."

"Your hair is thinning."

"Your teeth aren't white enough."

"You're overweight."

"What will you look like in ten years if you look like this now?"

"Who's going to want you?"

My mind moves from one default to the next, proclaiming lie after lie to myself. I then began to imagine what it would be like to be financially stable enough to get a few things done. You know just a little lift here and a little tuck there, possibly a cream for this and a cream for that.

I mean, what would be the big deal, if it's subtle enough? I'm not trying to look like a Picasso painting, I just want some natural modifications, if you will.

Along with this critical thinking, I had always felt like I was walking through life in cement shoes, slowly moving forward but often getting stuck with a misplaced heaviness that said, *there's something more* and *something isn't right, something is off.*

It was a feeling as though I had a missing purpose. It was a void that ate away at me, and there always seemed to be something on the back of my mind or even an elephant in the room, but it was more than just forgetting my lunch for work or telling myself I'll start my diet Monday. It was as though I had misplaced my identity and didn't know where to find it.

Have you ever cleaned and felt super proud and organized but then you go to find something and have no idea where it is because you cleaned? Now you're searching and searching for this lost item, and you can't find it. But where did I put it? It was a super important item. That's how it felt, I was searching for something I owned but couldn't find, no matter how messy or organized I seemed to be.

How could I be saved and yet feel far from God?

I didn't know how to walk without weight, anxiety, fear, and confusion. Where do I start? What am I supposed to do? How do I defeat the enemy when he keeps attacking me and if I can just be honest, I asked God why He seemed to hate me so much?

I felt unloved by God; it was like watching a movie featuring everyone else's blessings. I got to watch everyone enjoy things I strived for (so I thought) and glide through life without any major problems.

But that wasn't true, it was just how it seemed. I was watching life pass me by, while looking through one of those fun mirrors at the fair. My sight was distorted. My mind was running a race that I couldn't keep up with, and I decided it was time to fight. I took a leap of faith and tried something I had never tried before, and that's when God began a work in me.

Then, the time came to be unveiled (2 Corinthians 3:16-18 NLT) to have a relationship with Jesus that was fruitful. It was time to find the plans God had for my life as I overcame each obstacle and learned that He never leaves me or forsakes me (Hebrews 13:5, Joshua 1:9 NLT).

Eventually, God spoke to me after an experiential prayer saying, "Stop looking in the mirror and giving the enemy power because your self-destruction is hindering you from the things that I need you to do."

God began to walk me through one of the most emotional times in my life and taught me how to be a Christian. His work in me didn't begin when I was in a good place, but rather a major transition and life change was about to take place. It would have been convenient to learn who I was in Christ and be guided through a joyful, happy, and much easier time in my life. But God is not a god of convenience, and I wonder, would I have listened if I wasn't being propelled into this new chapter of life.

I knew there had to be other women scratching their heads, feeling lost. I remember reading about Moses and his people wandering for forty years and thinking, *What a bunch of idiots, who wanders for forty years?* To which God replied (not that I asked!) "Jaime, you're thirty-eight," and He just left that sitting there for me to stew in for a second. Touché Lord, Touché.

God told me long ago, "***Don't get inspired and get tired.***" You see, the problem is that women are going to church and getting inspired on Sunday and tired on Monday. How do you create purpose, heal, grow, teach, love, work, etc. and do life with Jesus and feel like you are not only doing it well but understanding it and doing enough to feel worthy?

You feel overwhelmed by the Bible. Wondering where do I start? You don't sound or act like other Christian women. You feel like there is too much to learn and not enough time in your day. You have chronic pain, your marriage is failing, your kids are driving you crazy, and you feel too stressed and too hurt. You literally feel too tired to be saved, too broken to be loved.

I said all of these things. I filled my mind with quotes, read Scripture, and even ignored God when I felt His pull and instead would watch HGTV while eating snacks at night when my daughter went down for bed because I felt as though I was entitled to it. I mean, what parent doesn't try to fit in a lifetime of "me time" after the kids go to bed? Guilty!

However, the enemy wants you distracted, stressed, and tired. If you're distracted, it takes you longer to get to your destination. So, let me just confide in you by telling you that I know. I've been there wandering for thirty-eight years! But God is still waiting on you, and while some destinations He had for you have passed, your purpose is still there. The beauty is that the destinations can change, but if you are in alignment, He moves you from glory to glory (2 Corinthians 3:18 ESV).

So, come with me as I do my best to, *AUTHENTICALLY* explain how I created a relationship with God that made me feel worthy. One that actually clicked! Because you'll never want to go back when that light bulb goes off, and the veil is removed. The old is gone, and the new has come (2 Corinthians 5:17 NLT).

CHAPTER ONE

Labeled

"**A**re you going to calm down?" My mother struggled to ask.
"NO!" I shouted.

The water was ice cold as it hit the back of my head. My stomach was aching because the sink and the edge of the countertop met together like a dagger that was jabbing into my stomach and into my ribs. My doctor had given my worn-out mother advice on how to calm my tantrums as a kid. His advice was to hold the back of my head under ice-cold water that flowed from a faucet until I calmed down.

Some of us are born with more wit and determination than others, and I definitely had them both. I remember asking my mother if I was adopted or if I had a twin that passed away because while I was loved by my mother and siblings, I never felt complete. Obviously, if I had been adopted, I could know without a doubt that there was, in fact, a missing piece.

If this were the case, I would feel better and be complete. But that wasn't the answer to the problem. I was told I was "bad, naughty, evil, crazy" these words pelted me like daggers, and while I don't remember being told I was smart or pretty until later in life, I do remember without a doubt being "bad."

Looking back, I know there was a spiritual connection even at such a young age. Yes, I believe spirits can attach themselves to children. Jesus healed children of demon possession in the Bible (Mark 9:14-27 NLT). I don't believe I was possessed, I believe I was oppressed along with a strong temperament that I can sometimes have today. (Bless my heart and those around me.) The difference is that I know as an adult who I am in Christ, and I know how the enemy wants to attack me.

A possession is either of the enemy or of God. You can have the possession of provision from God or possession of a demon. One will bear good fruit, and the other will not. I think you can guess which one does not bear good fruit, and which one does. You've guessed right. Of God, equals good fruit, and not of God equals bad fruit.

The definition of possession is the state of having, owning, or controlling something. Therefore, if a demon possesses you, it will control you.

Being oppressed by definition is being burdened spiritually or mentally or weighed heavily upon. This is something the devil enjoys doing. Oppression for adults is: depression, sexism, extreme fear, anxiety, and nightmares, which are just a few. Oppression for a child is: feeling extremely overwhelmed all the time, extreme fear, anxiety, nightmares, extreme tantrums that happen often, or feeling like something is always with you or watching you, etc.

Wait a minute, those are similar to adult symptoms. Yes, and that's because the Holy Spirit is the Holy Spirit, and a demon is a demon. You don't get baby versions just because you're a kid. Kids can't communicate what is happening a lot of the time. Heck, sometimes we can't communicate what is happening. Ever had PMS symptoms? I don't know about you, but I sure have felt oppressed and unable to express myself properly when I have a fluctuation in hormones. Even though I know hormones from PMS are not oppression but a group of medical symptoms, the point is the lack of control in our emotions that can lead to taking it too far.

I think we can forget as adults that we don't always express ourselves the right way and that we sometimes lose sight of how to engage a situation in a healthy way. Just don't do what my ex-husband used to do and lay your hand on your spouse's forehead and chant, "The power of Christ compels you!" I promise it will get you nowhere. Was it funny? Yes, but did he risk his safety? Yes.

I was a normal happy kid who was oppressed in a home with past spiritual connections from ancestors, as well as being in a home with an emotionally/mentally absent father and an extremely expressive and stressed out nurturing mother causing a confusing home with a lot of chaos. Everyone in the home was under spiritual warfare, but there was no one in the home to fight it.

However, nothing was controlling me to the point of being unable to be happy a lot of the time or to have normal child-like moments. Therefore, I was not possessed. (I'm sure if you ask my mother, she would find me not being possessed, debatable.)

You're probably thinking about your two-year-old child and wondering if the terrible twos are part of what I'm speaking of, and it's not. Trust me, I've been there with my kids for the terrible twos, horrible threes, and horrendous fours.

Oppression goes beyond a two-year-old being sad and crying because he can't say, "cookie" or you handed him the red cup and how dare you because he wanted the blue one. Lord, help us.

My point is that on top of the oppression, there was condemnation. You see, a child acts on what they watch. A child identifies with what they hear. If you tell a child, "Shame on you," then they learn to feel shame which the Bible says in Romans 10:11 (ESV) "For the Scripture says, "Everyone who believes in Him will not be put to shame." When Jesus died, our shame went with Him.

Your thoughts are what you feel, and what you feel is what you do. (Read that again). If I'm a young adult and I'm told that I'm not smart, I will then begin (if I'm not confident enough) to think about everything that is wrong to make me unintelligent; once I think about those things, I begin to feel not good enough or even stupid. I may begin to talk down to myself, which is my do, and my do can lead to not attending college, delaying my calling, not applying for certain jobs or obsessing over being "dumb," and possibly even start to feel depressed, etc.

So, I *HEARD* I wasn't smart, I now *THINK* I'm not smart, which made me *FEEL* not good enough, so I *DID* an action based on my thought and feeling that led me to talk down to myself or drop out of college. Your thoughts are what you feel, and what you feel is what you do.

So, what happens when we put that into a positive scenario? I *HEARD* I'm beautiful, and that makes me *THINK* I'm beautiful, and that makes me *FEEL* healthy, confident, and happy, and because I feel that way, I *CAN* talk positive to myself, walk taller, socialize more, and spread that positive nature onto others.

Proverbs 4:23 (GNT) says, "Be careful how you think; your life is shaped by your thoughts,"

Proverbs 23:7 says, (AMP) "For as he thinks in his heart, so is he."

God spoke everything into existence in the beginning, and He SPOKE life into creating the earth, so we too should speak life into ourselves and those around us.

Proverbs 18:21 (ESV) says, "Death and life are in the power of the tongue, and those who LOVE IT will eat its fruit."

I know what you're thinking. That last Scripture has to be off because you don't LOVE to speak that way to yourself, your spouse, or your kids and you wouldn't be wrong. It feels awful. But do you hate it enough to change it?

Ok, but how are you supposed to have a marriage that's breaking down, deal with past hurts, raise kids that need every ounce of you, keep a clean house and speak life into others and yourself. Who signed you up for this?

You did! You signed up for it when you accepted Jesus as your Lord and Savior, and He died for you to give it to Him. Everything you do comes back to His death and sacrifice. If it doesn't, then His death was for nothing.

He said to not worry but instead pray about everything. Not for some things, but everything. Tell Him what you need because, let's be honest, He knows anyway. Then, thank Him for all He has done, and only then will you experience God's peace. Not your peace, but God's peace.

I'm not saying that knowing who you are in Christ will automatically fix everything in your life. What it will do is give you a sense of peace in the chaos. It will give you something to cling on too and knowing who you are will help you as you walk out the difficult times.

Proverbs 16:24 (NLT) reads, "Kind words are like honey, sweet to the soul and healthy for the body."

Speaking kind words is literally healthy for your entire BODY! Therefore, kind words to someone else are healthy for their body. It doesn't say that kind words are healthy for a hand or a foot, no, it says the body.

When you begin to change your heart, you begin to have a heart of God. His desires become your desires, which exceed anything we can understand. We won't always know what God is doing, how He is working in our lives, or the timing it takes, but He can provide His peace that will guard your heart and mind as you live in Christ Jesus. So, you see, my friends. We have to live in Christ Jesus.

Your time with Him has to become a desire that you hold within you. I know our seasons are so different, sometimes changing quickly or staying too long, especially if we have kids or work 40+ hours a week.

Priscilla Shirer mentions in one of her sermons that even as a full-time pastor, she had three kids in sports, homework to help with, and made sure to cook dinner every night when she was home, and this was a season where she didn't get time with the Lord as she would have liked too.

If the woman who was in a movie about a war room didn't have every waking hour to spend with God, then what are we doing condemning ourselves and making excuses?

Here we are walking around thinking that because we don't have enough time to give Him, we just won't give Him anything, telling ourselves that there's too much to pray for, and we don't have time to say it all. God doesn't want you to hide because you're overwhelmed. He said come to me all who are burdened, and I will give you rest. (Matthew 11:28 NLT).

So, what did Priscilla do? She picked a Scripture each week that she felt God was leading her to and put it everywhere. In her car, her bathroom mirror, her desk, and even in the kitchen and she would read it throughout the day, as it was always within arm's reach. And that is how you meditate on God's Word and keep Gods Word on your heart in a busy season.

You can find time within moments to just pray or speak to Him. Even if it's in the car on the way to work, and even if it's a prayer of thanksgiving right before you drift off for a nap because you finally got a baby to sleep, then that's ok too.

But, just like brushing your teeth and taking a shower (which is a great place to talk to God as well), He wants you to think of Him and have it become who you are since you are, after all, one with Him.

I know that you are probably thinking about the fact that you have young children, so you're trying to accept this as your reason for the next eighteen years. But we also cannot stay stagnate in our relationship with Him.

So, let's start here. Give yourself the grace you have been gifted. Don't look in that mirror and give the enemy power. If a negative thought comes into your mind, immediately catch it and release it. Replace it with God's truth. Tell yourself right now, *"I AM BEAUTIFUL."* Even if you don't feel it right away, it's ok. You have to start, and I believe the foundation for healthy minds is what we speak. It's one of the places the enemy likes to attack me, so it's something I have to weed often.

Just the other day, I had a photo taken of me, and it was the worst angle possible. I looked like I had a shrunken head and a swollen body. The photo made me look disproportionate, and it bothered me. So, I understand that sometimes it happens, and to make matters worse, we live in a world with social media at our finger tips, and our lives are shared with everyone.

So why should we start this book with our minds and how we speak?

The Bible says in Ephesians 3:17 (TPT), "Then, by constantly using your faith, the life of Christ will be released inside of you, and the resting place of His love will become the very source and root in your life."

How beautiful is that? It says by constantly using your faith, not sometimes but constantly. So, always be speaking to Him as if He is your Father or best friend, and by finding a relationship with Him, you will become rooted.

Whatever you were told as a child, a teen, co-worker, spouse, or whatever you are telling someone else that isn't of God. Stop it. Start replacing what the enemy has been doing and take back your life.

Ephesians 4:22-24 (TPT) reads:

> "And He has taught you to let go of the lifestyle of
> the ancient man, the old self-life, which was cor-
> rupted by sinful and deceitful desires that spring
> from delusions. Now, it's time to be made new by
> every revelation that's been given to you and to be
> transformed as you embrace the glorious Christ-
> within as your new life and live in union with Him!
> For God has recreated you all over again in his per-
> fect righteousness, and you now belong to him in
> the realm of true holiness."

Your void, ache, stress, and tension seem messy, but He wants it all. So, speak life into your home and family and set new rules for yourself, your children, and your spouse. Start by thanking Jesus for things, and then remember that through Him, you are able to love yourself for all the small moments you overlook. Proceed to thank your children for the things they do and have them be thankful. Big changes come from small efforts.

If not, then devastation can set in, and nobody wants that. I remember my aunt asking me when I was about ten years old what I wanted to be when I grew up, and I excitedly said, "A model!" She smirked, patted me on the back, and said, "Oh honey, why don't you do something different instead." I was only ten, but I could feel at that moment that I wasn't pretty enough to be a model.

Later in life, around fifteen, that same aunt was talking to me and asked what I wanted to go to college for, and I replied, "A dental hygienist." She gave that same smirk and a pat on the back and said, "Oh, you don't want to look inside people's mouths all day, do you?" So, I decided at that moment that I didn't want to look inside people's mouth's all day. In reality, I wanted to be a hygienist really badly. I would have been good at it and enjoyed it.

Did my aunt mean to do that? No, she didn't, but what happens is *we take the things that we dislike, and project them into advice,* and we don't take into account that we could be hindering someone from something that they really want to try or are even called to do by being negative with our actions and words.

Does that mean that you don't guide your children into what you think they would be good at? Well, no, but you also have to remember that your child changes throughout growing up and that your desire for their life might not be God's calling for them.

My point is that it takes but a moment and a few words to mislead someone who has no one to talk too or lacks confidence.

So, if you find yourself in a moment when you realize you shouldn't have said something, then go to that person and correct it. You may think that it's minor, but it probably isn't. Simple can hurt too.

Prayer

Jesus,

I need you. I don't speak kindly to myself or to others, and it's hindering my life. I want to live in the fullness you have promised me by seeking you with prayer and thanksgiving. You didn't make a mistake when you made me; instead, you made me fearfully and wonderfully. Help me to renew my mind by using words that are pleasing to you. I lay down my anxious mind, stress, and emotions for you to take. I nail them to the cross where they belong. Help me along this journey as I discover who I am in you. Speak to me boldly so I can know your love for me and with that love, go out into the world and be the light that you so graciously have chosen me to be.

In Jesus' Name, Amen

CHAPTER 2
WHO AM I?

*L*ove me for me. Have you ever said that to someone? Have you ever felt like you couldn't figure out who you were, and then to make things more frustrating, you would hear people say, "Know who you are in Christ." Cool, thanks Becky, but how?

We've gone over the importance of speaking because death and life are in the power of the tongue. But how do we figure out who we are in Christ? What does that mean, and what does knowing look like?

I had all of these questions. For years, I felt like I would ask God to show me who I was in Christ, and the only thing He would reveal to me was the word "precious," I loved that word. Nobody had ever told me I was precious before, and I understood God's love behind it, but I wanted more. A definite drawn-out, YES! I am this and that, and without a doubt, know it. But I just couldn't.

What do you think of when you think of something precious? I know for me, I think of a puppy or a baby, so you're probably not thinking of yourself as an adult when you hear the word precious. God sees us as His children; therefore, my ABBA thinks I'm precious. It was a beautiful place to start.

You may have heard something similar when you asked God who you were in Christ and received an answer like loved, beloved, sanctified, or renewed. Those are all beautiful and truthful things, but how do we dig more into them? What does it mean, and does God do that to make us grow into who we are? To seek and find or to knock and it will be opened? I believe the answer to that is, yes.

I think it's important to remind ourselves about what the Word of God says happened when we gave our life to Christ.

- I am re-created (2 Corinthians 5:17)
- I am free (Galatians 5:1)
- I am redeemed/restored (Ephesians 4:22-24)
- I have the mind of Christ (1 Corinthians 2:16)
- I am gifted (1 Peter 4:10)
- I am powerful (2 Timothy 1:7)
- I am no longer a slave (Galatians 4:7)
- I am God's heir (Galatians 4:7)
- I am valuable (Luke 12:6-7)
- I OVERCOME! (Revelation 12:11 AMP)

You are so many things in Christ, especially an over-comer. Jesus has a testimony, and so do you. Think about it: without Jesus' testimony, we wouldn't follow Him and we wouldn't have anything to hang onto.

Your testimony and mine need to be heard to bring others to our Savior. That's why you go through things. If you want to follow someone with good morals and values, there are plenty of options, but it's His sacrifice that makes the deal. We are one with Him, and because of His blood and testimony, we are able to defeat the enemy!

Your testimony is unique to you in the way that you can use the good and the bad to help other people. We don't have mountains to keep us down we have mountains to show others how to climb.

You can use Scripture after Scripture to try and call people to Christ, but sometimes it's not until you connect with them on a personal level, letting them know that you're a human who has been through the valley, that they will begin to let their guard down and listen to you.

I used to say to my ex-husband, "Love me for me!" I mean, I would cry it out. I needed him to stop trying to push me into what I felt like was a completely different person. I would feel so unloved and confused while he was one of those people who knew exactly who he was. I don't mean in Christ but who he was as a walking talking human. He knew his ticks, thought process, style, strengths, and everything. He would respond to me by saying, "Well, then, who are you, tell me?" And I couldn't.

This is why I wanted to talk to you about speaking life first because the lack of confidence and the identity we hold onto as children and then struggling adults hinders who we know we are in Christ. I could fill this book with everything God says we are. What it boils down to is that we have been given a new mind. We have been given a new way of life and are to walk in it.

I grew up in an aggressive house, and my mother swore all of the time. We spoke disrespectfully, sarcasm was a must, and while we did give out compliments, we also picked each other apart. I didn't realize the severity of it until I became saved. (I still struggle with a couple swear words to this day).

For instance, one day, I'm heading to the bathroom at church, and I'm pretty sure I stiff-armed an eighty-year-old to get into the bathroom faster; I mean, we all know how the lines get after service lets out, so cut me some slack.

I'm waiting in line, and a woman comes in after me, and we have to wait maybe a minute or two, not long at all. Two stalls open up at the same time, and she looks at me and says, "Praise God, He is so good a stall has opened up."

WHAT? Lady, you knew it would! You came in here to use the bathroom!

God didn't open the stall for you, someone had finished and come out. Yes, praise Him in all things, but my goodness, you're making me look bad. I totally condemned myself at that moment and felt like I wasn't Christian enough because I didn't talk that way about everything.

"Oh, praise God, my Lord, a parking spot has opened close to the entrance!" Pull in, Karen! You've been circling for five minutes, you could have been inside four times now.

Why didn't I think or speak like these women? What was wrong with me?

Nothing, absolutely nothing. I was flawed, yes, and still am, but nothing is wrong with you or me.

I remember being at church and seeing Lisa Bevere Speak for the first time, and I was so excited because I had read some of her books, and she seemed very bold in her writing, and I loved that. I loved her testimony.

She stood up there and walked across that stage like even a bolt of lightning couldn't take her down. She spoke with such certainty and had this tone to her voice that was firm and strong. She was funny and had style. She wrote books and preached God's Word on stage, and I thought she was everything I wanted to be.

So, I said to God, "I want that!" Unfortunately, I continued to struggle with who I was, and God wouldn't answer my request for five. Long. years.

SILENCE

A silent retreat? What in the world was a silent retreat? My friend kept posting about them, so I finally messaged her and asked.

She sent me all the info, and I couldn't have been more intrigued. But, could I do it? This retreat didn't seem very retreat-ish at all.

I mean, I think of a spa or something when I think of retreat. However, the definition of a retreat doesn't quite line up with a spa when we think of it in the light of massages and cucumbers over the eyes, but rather a retreat is an act of moving back or withdrawing.

At this silent retreat, I would be taking a vow of silence to God for 48 hours away from family, cell phones, computers, the news, or the radio. I mean everything and anything that connected you to the outside world.

I'm a mother of three at this point, and I have separation anxiety from my children when they are young; while my older two were grown, I had one peanut left.

How in the world would I get through not hearing or seeing my youngest for 48 hours? I mean, she was only three years old, and it's the longest I have ever been away from her.

But I had to. Life was propelling me forward on a ride I couldn't control. Well, I couldn't control what was happening, but I could control the outcome on my end by coming together with God and taking control of my life.

My ex-husband filed for divorce in August 2021, and I went on my silent retreat in October 2021, knowing that I had to. God was calling me too, and I needed to hear from Him because when life throws things at you, you need God to catch them.

The experience at this retreat was life-changing. It was like nothing I had ever experienced. People fast from food and Facebook but to take a vow of silence and just sit in nature. Who does that?

Well, Jesus did. Mark 1:35 (TPT) says, "The next morning, Jesus got up long before daylight, left the house while it was dark, and made his way to a secluded place to give himself to prayer."

Luke 6:12 (TPT) says, "After leaving the synagogue, Jesus went into the high hills to spend the whole night in prayer to God."

Luke 5:16 (NIV) says, "But Jesus often WITHDREW to lonely places and prayed."

What was a retreat again? It's withdrawing.

We are so busy getting ourselves worked up over the news and other people's drama, work, and so much more. Maybe life is a mess, and you need to get away from the noise, but maybe life is good, and you just need to know how to become closer to God. If that's you, then maybe a silent retreat would be good for you. Actually, not maybe but rather I know it will be good for you.

In my opinion, you can't just go to any silent retreat; you need one that is Christian based and held together by like-minded people who will pray for you and intercede in your life.

I was sitting in my room at the retreat in silence on the second day reading the Word of God, and I began to remember what I had said to God five years before about Lisa Bevere.

My God is so awesome that He's going to remind me of a moment, a tiny comment I made to Him five years prior. It's mind-blowing.

As I began to remember everything about Lisa and what I wanted to be, her tone of voice, her walk, her words, and her knowledge. God says to me, "It's not her tone of voice, wisdom, or character you want. It's her confidence." I was like, "Oh, yeah, I don't have much of that."

The thing is that, the confidence God was talking about wouldn't be something I understood until a couple of months later while I was spending time with Him. You see, earthly confidence and godly confidence are two different things.

I wanted earthly confidence from a woman who had godly confidence, and I didn't know it. So, as I began to dive into the word confidence, I couldn't believe how many times the Bible mentioned confidence.

Ephesians 3:12 (TPT) reads, "We have boldness through him, and free access as kings before the Father because of our complete confidence in Christ's faithfulness."

Hebrews 13:6 (TPT) says, "So, we can say with great confidence: I know the Lord is for me and I will never be afraid of what people may do to me."

Isaiah 32:17 (NLT) says, "And this righteousness will bring peace. Yes, it will bring quietness and confidence forever."

Confidence comes from God, His Word, and a relationship with Him. As we grow in Him and equip ourselves, we grow in His confidence. Even being strong and courageous like He commands us to do will take confidence that we can only get through Him and knowing who we are in Him.

You're probably thinking ok, ok, be confident in Him through prayer, relationship, and a renewing of my mind by speaking life not only into me but into others, and my faith comes by hearing and hearing by the Word of God. I've got it. So, what are my next steps in learning who I am in Christ?

Well, my friend, along with all of that awesomeness, you can define your identity in Christ through your Spiritual Gifts, Strengths, Core Values, and the Five-Fold Ministry.

Prayer

Abba,

thank you that through you I am powerful, gifted, and valuable with a mind of Christ, and I pray that any words that were spoken over me that go against your will for me will be broken away in Jesus' name! Thank you that anything simple or harsh that was spoken to me no longer hinders me. Lord, fill my mouth with a tongue that builds up and doesn't tear down. Give me the confidence to be bold in my walk with you.

In Jesus' name, Amen

CHAPTER 3
Spiritual Gifts and Attacks

*I*used to pretend as a kid that I could move things with my mind. I would even have dreams about it. In my dreams, I could close doors with a wave of my hand. Basically, the T.V. series, Stranger Things is a glimpse into my imagination as a kid.

My friend and I would talk about it, and she revealed to me that her aunt could light a candle by just thinking about it, and so, like an idiot, I would stare at candles sometimes. I thought if I could choose one super-power, it would definitely be to move things with my mind. However, most of us have witnessed what happened in the 1976 horror film; *Carry* and that didn't work out too well.

I still have a very creative and imaginative mind. However, things have happened to me spiritually that have not been imagined.

We used to live in this old house, old meaning over a hundred years old. I remember the first time I was spiritually attacked, I was paralyzed with fear. Unfortunately, every other time was also paralyzing. While I was oppressed, I had never been attacked in this way until about ten years old.

I remember I was sleeping, and I began to have a dream that I'll never forget, and it started with children playing on a merry-go-round and laughing. It suddenly switched to frogs on lily pads making croaking sounds. Eventually, the dream began to switch between the children laughing and the frogs croaking. Faster and faster, they switched between the images.

Laughter to croaking again and again until finally I was woken up by an intense pressure, I couldn't move or speak. I tried to scream, but I couldn't, and I was more terrified than I had ever been in my life. I felt as though the pressure physically propelled my upper body off the bed. It was as if something had gone in and then out of my upper body.

That night I was spiritually attacked, and it wasn't the last time it would happen. Throughout my life, I was attacked, and while there would be times it didn't happen for months, there were times it would happen often, leaving me in fear of sleeping at times in my life. I believe the enemy would attack me while I was sleeping and even wake me as a kid. My mother would find me in the middle of the living room, watching TV at two or three in the morning.

I had spells of insomnia so bad at some points in my life that at one low, low moment of desperation, I thought about taking my own life so that I could sleep. Just finally shut my eyes and rest because it had been weeks since I had slept, and I felt God wasn't helping me.

After slurring my words at work, I finally went to the doctors for insomnia, and they gave me all sorts of depression medications that didn't do anything as well as a sleep aid. At one point, I had an allergic reaction to an anxiety med that caused an E.R. visit. On the nights that I couldn't sleep, I would feel as though my body was resting, but my mind was awake. My heart would be racing while my eyes were so desperate and tired that they would just move from side to side as though they were searching for rest even though they were closed.

One day I was sitting at my son's football practice with my mom and I felt this darkness come over me, and all of a sudden, I knew immediately that I wanted to take my life. I looked at my mother and very calmly asked if she would stay at the field while I went home for a nap because I was exhausted. I stood up, and left.

I don't remember the drive home or walking in the house, but I remember I held a bottle of Ambien that had no effects on my insomnia in my hand and knelt down on the side of my bed. I looked up at God and said, "I bet I would sleep now, wouldn't I"?

I said it as if to taunt Him, I said it as though I was going to punish God for not helping me. I was going to take every pill in that bottle.

We're so harsh towards people who take their own lives, but as you can see, it takes but a moment to seek relief in the wrong way.

The crazy thing is that God didn't send some angel down to slap the bottle of pills out of my hands. He didn't send some loud audible voice to command me to put it down. He did, however, flood me with images of my children.

I dropped the bottle and began to weep and then I just started repeating, "Thank you Jesus," over and over again. I began to do just that until I was saying, "Thank you, Jesus", faster than my mouth could keep up, and I began to laugh and giggle. My tears had turned from sad and worn out to happiness, and I felt lifted.

It took a couple more weeks for that awful spell of insomnia to lift and years of other prescription medications to sleep, but now I no longer take prescription medication to sleep. I do have some insomnia from time to time due to hormonal shifts or extreme stress in life that can hit us all during certain seasons, but I know what it is, and I know that stress can trigger it for me. I'm now aware, so when I dive deep into why I've had extreme insomnia in the past, I can pinpoint the reason which eliminates the fear.

For instance, I had to put a rule in place that my ex and I couldn't have serious conversations that may end up in an argument or any intense conversations past a certain time at night. They had to wait until the next day because if I got anxious from those intense conversations, then I couldn't sleep. My mind is creative, and I would just ponder and ponder and be wide awake while Mr. Snores-a-lot was sound asleep.

The enemy doesn't want me rested. He hasn't since I was a kid. He hates me. He hates you. He hates what God needs me to do. He hates what God is calling *YOU* to do. So, we must learn who we are so that we can be aware of how He likes to attack us.

The last time I was attacked was in October 2021 on my silent retreat. I was already nervous as I don't like to sleep in places that I don't know. On the first night of the retreat, I climbed into bed. I dozed off and was awoken by a strong pressure that held me down. I couldn't speak or move. My blanket rose over me, and as I tried to scream for Jesus (to stop the attack) the blanket came down over me like the entity was trying to smother me with the blanket. The blanket literally possessed the shape of a hand as if someone's whole arm and hand was coming up to suffocate me. Then just as suddenly as it came, it went, but it felt like forever.

I immediately sat up, turned the light on, and began to read the Word of God, but because I was so tired, I had to put the Bible down and just rock in the rocking chair that was in the room so that I didn't fall back asleep.

I was startled, shocked, and even upset with God. I mean, I was on a silent retreat, and I'm literally taking a vow of silence as a fast to be closer to God. How could this happen here?

I was so tired, and I thought for sure that it was a one-time thing and that I could now try to go to sleep and that God would protect me. I grabbed my Bible and used it for a pillow, thinking for certain I would be shielded this way.

No longer did I dose off that I got attacked again! This time the pressure came from my upper back. No warning signs; it just hit, I tried to scream, but the pressure was so intense. I was trying to push out a scream so bad my throat hurt after it was over.

I sat up and I was now in complete distress, I had never been hit twice in a row like that, I wanted to pack my bags and leave. I was going to run out of there faster than I came. I was confused beyond measure and knew I couldn't go back to sleep.

The next morning, I wrote the intercessor (our prayer warriors assigned to each retreat) a note explaining that I had been attacked and that I was afraid to sleep. I explained this had been happening since I was a kid and that I was tired!

Later that day, I got a knock on my door. She showed me a note (the reason we are passing notes is that we obviously cannot speak with the vow we made) that asked if she could pray over me and my room. I immediately and gladly said yes, and she did just that, and then left.

I was given another note at lunch by the same woman and asked if I would be open to being prayed over by multiple people. I accepted that gift, and I believe about four to five women gathered around me and laid hands on me. They prayed over my entire body, moved their hands over my head, back, and legs, and at one point, a set of hands were placed on my upper back. I could feel their love and compassion as they prayed. I'm just sitting there crying in total faith and mercy at this moment.

I then felt a pull where the hands were placed on my upper back. The pull wasn't from the hands of the person praying behind me, it was that something left me through my upper back, which was the last place I had been attacked!

I went back to my room after I had been prayed over and just cried and cried. I was given a letter of encouragement from the creator of the silent retreat, assuring me that this was something that God allowed at this retreat so that I could be fully healed. That it was nothing I intentionally let in and more than likely was a generational entity that had been in my family for years, and it thought it could continue to torment me.

I was so moved by the letter that I cried out to God, "Why me, why not my sisters or my brother, why me, why am I attacked like this?" God responded immediately with, "No, not why me, but not me anymore." This led me to do that weird laugh-cry thing where you're now happy, but you can't stop ugly crying. I just kept repeating, "Thank you Jesus, not me anymore."

God allowed this to happen because He needed that entity (or possibly more of then I don't know) to leave so that I could do what He called me to do. I believe that entity was hindering me from my calling. If I hadn't been attacked, I wouldn't have been prayed over, which relieved me of the unclean spirit, which means I wouldn't be writing this.

I was free, but to keep it away, I had to remember Matthew 12:43-45 (TPT) which says:

> "When a demon is cast out of a person, it roams around a dry region, looking for a place to rest, but never finds it. Then it says, "I'll return to the house I moved out of." And so, it goes back, only to find that the house is vacant, warm, and ready for it to move back in. So, it goes looking for seven other demons more evil than itself, and they all enter together to live there. Then the person's condition becomes much worse than it was in the beginning. This describes what will also happen to the people of this evil generation."

Gross, a warm place to live in reference to us, does that sound creepy to anyone else? This Scripture is telling us that back sliding can have consequences. Many of us have never been delivered like this. Some of you might be reading this and thinking (in your Madea voice) *"Oh my Lort, what is in me!"*

Maybe many of you can relate to something like this and have even kept it to yourself for fear that no one would believe you. If the Holy Spirit is real and if all of the good and lovely things of the spirit realm are real, then I can assure you that evil is real too.

But we don't like to talk about it, or if we do, we tip toe and don't dive deep into real and scary spiritual attacks. I personally don't think that does anyone any good. I mean, what if your child has told you something like this, and you thought it was just their imagination? You need to be praying over them, their room, and fighting for them. You need to be speaking peace into your home and casting anything unholy or unclean out and now!

I always wondered why God seemed to forget me, why I wouldn't be delivered from things immediately when I would ask Him. Was it my lack of faith? I would ask God, "How big do you think a mustard seed is? You don't even think I have that!"

A few months after the silent retreat, I was reading in Mark and came across the story of the demon-possessed boy. The disciples were in distress because they could not cast this demon out. Jesus then responds with, "This type of powerful spirit can only be cast out by fasting and prayer." (Mark 9:29 TPT)

I literally almost jumped out of the chair. Where was I when I was delivered from this spirit? At a silent retreat, fasting and praying while surrounded by like-minded people who were also fasting and praying. BOOM! Bye evil.

But, can I tell you something? Before this retreat, I was luke-warm as a Christian. I was just going through the motions. God had done some work in me as a believer through classes that I had taken at church. I believed He was my Savior, and He even so mercifully healed me from some of the emotional decisions that I had made, but what He was really waiting for me to do was to give more of myself to Him.

I'm so sorry to tell you this, my beautiful friend, but you don't get to be delivered from something just because you go to church sometimes and have a coffee mug with a Scripture on it.

Listen to me, God has not forgotten you. His timing is not ours, and if I'm being honest, it's one of the most beautifully frustrating things on this planet. It is so hard in the moments when people are telling you your faith isn't strong enough. It's hard in the moments when you don't think you can take any more of what life is dishing out.

Even Jesus cried out to God when He stepped into the wilderness and asked God if there was any other way that He could free us, a plan B for His life before He accepted His calling, and then Jesus began to sweat so bad that the beads of sweat dropped like blood.

If Jesus really did sweat blood, I believe it was the confirmation that He was asking for, and God delivered, but not by taking His fear away. No, Jesus had to face His fear, but what did God confirm His question with? With blood! And what is Jesus? He's the living sacrifice and the blood covenant for our sins! God was saying, no, Jesus, there is no other way, and I'll prove it right now with blood.

If Jesus, our Lord and Savior, was so scared that He asked God for confirmation that maybe, just maybe, there was any other possible way, then we too can feel like our path is too hard. But, make no mistake that even after Jesus asked God if there was another way, he then submitted by saying, your will, not mine.

When Jesus was on the cross, what did He say? He said, "My God, My God, why have you forsaken me?" Can you imagine the pain and torment He endured?

I'm annoyed with a paper cut, for goodness sake. He had nails driven into Him, and thorns pushed into His skull while He hung there waiting and waiting for six hours after He had been beaten and ridiculed and continued to be ridiculed for you and I. And He wondered, HAVE I BEEN FORGOTTEN? God, where are you?

Was Jesus crying out a prophecy, yes, and Psalms 22:1 (ESV) reads, "My God, my God, why have you forsaken me? Why are you so far from saving me, from the words of my groaning?"

But, don't you think he did wonder, "How much longer?"

Look at what Job went through. He lost everything. This is one of the hardest testimonies in the Bible next to Jesus. If a man named Job went through what he did and was so loyal to God that God referred to him as blameless, then what hope do the rest of us have?

While that isn't true, it's often how I feel when I read Job. I mean, this loyal man was allowed by God to be tormented by Satan.

God allowed for a test in order to strengthen my faith. Even a blameless man like Job had work to do. I had to face fear once more to see the truth. To see that God has His hand on me, and it's important to face the truth because it sets you free. God wanted me to see the power of prayer, he wanted me to start using it and to know my authority.

I could have run out of the retreat in fear. Even Jesus could have decided it was too much for Him to take. Job could have turned his back on God. But, this time, I chose to stay and fight.

There are so many people mad at God, and I don't care what I'm about to say next because I promised to be authentic, and that's that I too have yelled, cursed, and turned my back on God because I was weak and without a relationship with Him.

27

I said my prayers at night, listened to only Christian music, went to church, even did devotionals, and prayed with my children. What was His problem?

My will is not God's, and without knowing my purpose and aligning my life to be unveiled, I'll continue to wonder. This doesn't mean that an unveiling is pure bliss without any troubles in life. I'm not spreading sprinkles and glitter here.

The favor in our lives as followers of Christ is something to look at from all angles. Take Mary, the mother of Jesus, for instance; can you imagine what she went through? We think it's so amazing and awesome that Mary got to carry Jesus, and it is, but that's the favor she had in her life. That favor had Joseph attached to it, and she was probably nervous that she would lose her future husband. That favor didn't get her to a birthing place at a palace, no, your girl rode on a donkey (put me on a donkey while I'm pregnant and about to give birth and see what happens to you) to a less than elegant barn and on to birth a king while another king was on the hunt to kill her baby!

That same favor would lead her to witness her son being crucified. Yet, still all part of the original favor. What an honor to raise Jesus, but what a hard life it must have been.

Jesus said it's hard to follow Him. At times it is. At times I've even said, "Is it worth it?" But we are borrowing this body. This is not our home. It is our job. His death gave us life, and we were given gifts as His people. (Ephesians 4:7)

Spiritual Gifts

Now that we have discussed some of the oppression that can have us bound (I'll have more of that to come), we can talk about the gifts that God has so graciously given us so that we may equip ourselves to bring Heaven to earth, shinning our light so other people can see and follow the life that Jesus has intended for them. They are as follows:

- **Administration**: Greek meaning is "to steer" this gift is to organize, direct and instill plans to lead others in the church. (1 Corinthians 12:28)
- **Apostleship**: Plant new ministries by going into places where the gospel cannot be preached; they are often encouragers and risk takers talented at multitasking. (Ephesians 4:11-14)
- **Craftsmanship**: Skilled at working with raw materials like wood, cloth, paints, etc., they are gifted to be creative for ministry. (Acts 18:2-3)
- **Discernment**: To distinguish between the presence of God, Satan, the world, and the flesh. To distinguish between spirits (Acts 5:1-11)
- **Evangelism**: To bring the good news of Jesus Christ and shout it to all who will hear. (Acts 8:5-6)
- **Exhortation:** A "how-to person" very practical with a desire to teach. A motivator with a plan. (Acts 14:22)
- **Faith:** Shows God's power in ways that create joy, hope, and encouragement for others. Faith that never dulls. (Acts 11:22-24)
- **Giving**: You are aware of the needs that He wants, and you meet them through giving. (Romans 12:8)
- **Healing:** Through you, God miraculously brings healing and deliverance from things like, disease and or infirmity. (Acts 3:1-10)
- **Helps:** A behind-the-scenes worker who helps to get things done and works joyfully, making life easier for those around them. (Acts 9:36)

- **Hospitality**: Serving others without a need for acknowledgment and doing it joyfully. (1 Peter 4:9)
- **Intercession**: Uses prayer with a confidence that can come only from God and uses that confidence to intercede on behalf of an individual or group. (Hebrews 7:25)
- **Knowledge**: understanding things of this world that are rooted in Scripture. Can retain the truth and know Scripture. (1 Corinthians 12:8)
- **Leadership**: To lead others into a deeper relationship with God and love them along the way. (Romans 12:8)
- **Mercy**: To sense and respond to the emotional and spiritual needs of others (Mark 9:41)
- **Miracles**: God-given ability to perform special signs that bring light and testify to God and His Word. (Acts 19:11-12)
- **Pastor**: Someone who is called to oversee, teach and guide a congregation and equip believers to do ministry work. (John 10:1-18)
- **Prophecy**: To apply the Word of God to a situation so that sin can be exposed. A deep capacity to trust God and hear His voice. (1 Thessalonians 1:5)
- **Teacher:** A gift given to communicate the truths of the Bible to others. They explain the meaning, proclamation, context, and application to the hearer's life. (1 Corinthians 12:28)
- **Tongues**: the ability to speak in a language unknown to the speaker. (Acts 2:1-13)
- **Wisdom:** the understanding of God's Word and His commandments, which leads to a righteous perspective. (1 Corinthians 12:8)
- **Service:** Overall goal of having a Christ-centered strength to do any task by serving. (Romans 12:7)

As you can see, these beautiful gifts are sprinkled through out the Bible, but we can find a handful right in Romans 12:6-8 (NLT) which reads:

> "In his grace, God has given us different gifts for doing certain things well, so if God has given you the ability to prophesy, speak out with as much faith as God has given you. If your gift is serving others, serve them well. If you are a teacher, teach well. If your gift is to encourage others, be encouraging. If it is giving, give generously. If God has given you leadership ability, take the responsibility seriously. And if you have a gift for showing kindness to others, do it gladly."

I know what you're thinking, "Girl! What is all of this?"

But, do you see? This is why I have to write this book and shout from the rooftops about all that you have been given. You are gifted with a purpose and more than just one Word from God. You are called to be thoroughly equipped for all God's good works.

You might read through these and see that a lot of them apply to you. We are all given these gifts, I know that can sound confusing but the Holy Spirit distributes them accordingly.

1 Corinthians 12:29-31 reads:

> "Are we all apostles? Are we all prophets? Are we all teachers? Do we all have the power to do miracles? Do we all have the gift of healing? Do we all have to ability to speak in unknown languages? Do we all have the ability to interpret unknown languages?

Of course not! SO YOU SHOULD EARNESTLY
DESIRE THE MOST HELPFUL GIFTS."

I don't have craftsmanship skills (Sure, I can learn to build something if I truly want to, but I don't have that desire), and if there was an athletic gift for God's glory, I can assure you He didn't give it to me. Now, if there was a gift for tripping over air, I've made it in God's kingdom.

So, while you may see yourself in a lot of them, God has actually made you like Liam Neeson and given you a special set of skills. (If you don't know who Liam Neeson is and what I'm referring to, then I'm sorry, I write my own jokes.)

Look at it this way, I can sing in worship to God, but I am not called to sing as a worship leader for God's glory. I promise, I do not have a voice like Fergie and Jesus.

My Gifts of the Spirit are; Prophecy, Mercy, Word of Knowledge, Exhortation, and Discernment.

1 Corinthians 12:4-6 (NIV) reads:

> "There are different kinds of gifts, but the same Spirit
> distributes them. There are different kinds of ser-
> vice, but the same Lord. There are different kinds
> of working, but in all of them and in everyone it is
> the same God at work."

You're probably wondering how you might go about finding out which ones God has so beautifully and graciously given to you.

I'm going to recommend two ways of finding out. One way is to go all in and not just find out your gifts from God but to dive into past hurts (By giving them to God). To surround yourself with like-minded people who are equipped and have been trained as God's servants to help you excel at your highest potential. Now, not all healing comes from your community, all of that comes from your relationship with Jesus, and through Him comes a relationship with other people who can help us. Please remember that we are here reading this, and I'm writing this because we have been wracking our brains trying to figure out what's out there for us.

So, what will set you apart from *KNOWING* but doing *NOTHING?*

God told me a while ago, as I was sitting on the edge of my bed daydreaming about ministering to someone, "Knowing and wisdom are two different things. What's the point of knowing if you don't use it wisely?" He was telling me to take my own advice that I was picturing myself giving. Isn't it easier to pick someone else up than it is ourselves?

I found out what my Spiritual Gifts were from joining a community called Kallah. Now, you won't just find a spiritual gifts assessment hanging out on their website Kallahculture.com at this moment, but you will find a tab labeled "Events," and when you click that, you have a few options and I recommend exploring them.

What the heck does Kallah mean? Jesus spoke Aramaic which is a form of Hebrew and kallah means bride or completion.

My life transformed when I went to my first *Come Away with Me* silent retreat, and yours will, too. From there, I dove into what's called, *The Unveiling Intensive*. It's at the intensive that you will go through multiple assessments to hone in on who you are. God will reveal why you are the way you are. He'll bring light to questions you've possibly had for a long time. But, remember you're reading this because you want more and to not stay stagnant.

The second way to find out your Spiritual Gifts is to go to giftstest.com, there are probably hundreds of assessments out there, but they will vary. So, these are the two that I would recommend.

Remember, Jesus went away and withdrew to connect and take Himself out of the chaos of life.

I highly recommend that you try out giftstest.com to start your journey. Even if you decide to use Kallah as your stepping stone to finding out who you are, you can begin here, and the sooner you start, the closer you become to affirming your identity in Christ.

List your Spiritual Gifts (from giftstest.com) here:

1.
_____

2.
_____

3.
_____

4.
_____

5.
_____

Prayer

Father,

Thank you for meeting me right where I'm at, you're always by my side. I praise you and thank you for your union and oneness with me. I do not have a spirit of fear but of love and of power and of a sound mind. Fear does not control me, nor is fear a part of who I am. I am strong and courageous like Joshua! You said you would cover me with your feathers, and under your wings will I find refuge. Thank you for your protection and covering. In Jesus' name, Amen

CHAPTER 4
Five-Fold Ministry

The Five-Fold Ministry is something I had never heard of until my time at the Intensive, and I feel that's because we are not being taught these things in the church. I feel that some churches will give a vague assessment when you become a member to hone in on where a good place is for you to serve in the church, and I think that's purposeful and wonderful. But, why don't we have classes on this? Why isn't anyone really breaking down how to find out exactly who we are in Christ?

I cannot say that all churches don't do this that would be a complete lie. There are many churches that focus on this. However, extensive classes on all things you and how to walk it out? Not as common as you would think, and I believe we are missing the ball on this as a church.

Churches have divorce care classes, abortion care classes, finance classes, grieving classes, and singles classes. We are equipping people to overcome hurts to excel in God's kingdom, and I have used many of the resources that churches have given, but classes on finding out who you are in Christ, I'm sorry, but I must have missed the memo.

If I take a divorce care class through church (which I have) but I have no idea who I am, then it's likely I may rush into another relationship and repeat the same mistakes (which I have).

I know I'm not the only one who missed the memo because God wouldn't have me writing a book about something that was so well known that there wasn't a need for it.

The five-fold helps the church by equipping Christians with what they need so that they can do God's will.

Let's dig into the Scripture in Ephesians 4:4-6 (TPT) that reads:

> "Being one body and one spirit, as you were all called into the same glorious hope of divine DESTINY. For the Lord God is one, and so are we, for we share in one faith, one baptism, and one Father. And He is the perfect Father who leads us all, works through us all, and in us all!"

Ephesians 4:9-13 (TPT) reads:

> "He "ascended" means that He returned to Heaven after He had first descended from the heights of Heaven, even to the lower regions, namely, the earth. The same one who descended is also the one who ascended above the heights of Heaven in order to begin the restoration and fulfillment of all things. He has appointed some with grace to be APOSTLES, some with grace to be PROPHETS, some with grace to be EVANGELISTS, some with grace to be PASTORS, and some with the grace to be TEACHER. And their calling is to nurture and prepare all the holy believers to do their OWN WORKS OF MINISTRY, and as they do this, they will enlarge and build up the body of Christ."

Then it continues on to say that the grace ministries will go on to build up the church until we secure oneness into faith and experience the fullness of God. So, I ask you again, why are we not teaching this in church? Because from what I can see, not only are we called to nurture our gifts but to prepare all believers.

In my opinion there is too much motivational speaking in the church. Do we need that, heck yes we do, but is there too much of it? Yes.

There is too much motivational speaking with out the teaching.

If you read this and don't feel that you're important in preparation for Jesus' return, you are not consuming this. There is a movement and a revival that needs to take place and you are called as a sister in Christ to be a part *OF* it and not apart *FROM* it. You were given a gift through grace with potential, appointed from the lover of your soul, to walk out in your destiny and bring Heaven to earth.

I wondered when I read these Scriptures why it says He gives us these things with, "grace". The Greek word "grace" is Charis. This word also means undeserving favor or gift and can also be used as charisma which is where we get the word charismatic. Chen is another word for grace, but in Hebrew, it means favor.

It's like when your child's birthday or Christmas comes around, and they are flooded with all of the wonderful things they don't need.

They're showered from the time they enter your womb. As you continue on in your pregnancy, you literally go on to have a baby shower and of course, from there you go onto every holiday. It's ok, it's fun, and while we could all cut back every Christmas and birthday, the point is that we give gifts. You give them because you love that person. You want to see the joy in their lives. They don't deserve one more stupid Lego for you to step on, risking your life and yelling things the Lord doesn't appreciate. Yet, here you are buying more just because little Tommy turned six, and well, it's better than video games.

We too give gifts, not because they deserve or earned them but because we love them. He gifted us these works so that we could lead people to Him making His sacrifice meaningful because He loves us.

You could literally change it from grace to; He GIFTED some apostle, He GIFTED some prophet, and so on. How beautiful is that!

The Five-Fold Ministry is:

APOSTLE: Awaken people to their God-designed potential. They help people discover who they are; they love to lead people, direct them, and watch them sprout into who God has called them to be.

PROPHET: They can hone in on God's truth and what God's heart is trying to convey; they can also direct people through hearing and learning the voice of God.

EVANGELIST: They love to deliver God's Word and act as vessels to help people experience Jesus and all He is. They walk in the way they believe you should live.

PASTOR: Shepard's who guide and bring healing. They are the tour guide of the Word of God, leading you through brokenness back to wholeness. They bring enjoyment to God's ministry.

TEACHER: They bring knowledge and destroy confusion, bringing the truth of God to each person's life to help them see how it applies to their lives as well.

When assessing your five-fold, it's important to know that you should find your top two gifts to focus on, which will enhance and customize our ability to bring who we are to full fruition. Again, you may see some qualities of yourself in more than one.

Remember, Scripture says He has given some apostles, some prophets, some evangelists, some pastors, and some teachers. You can focus on your top two while knowing each one independently. My top two are *prophet* and *pastor*.

You may have had people tell you that you possess some of these qualities or even experienced things that have made you wonder if you had gifts.

I've known since I was nineteen that I wanted to write. I just didn't know back then that I would one day give my life to Christ and be writing for His glory.

I've started many books and never finished them because I didn't have enough confidence in myself. I felt like I was supposed to do this thing that made me so very happy and gave me meaning, and was my dream, but the lack of confidence I had that I would even be successful or that anyone would buy one of my books beside my sisters and mother was so far-fetched that I would allow the enemy to win.

When I was at my first silent retreat, I was blessed enough to attend with one of my beautiful friends, and when I arrived on the first day and began to check out my room, I noticed my friend had left a book on the bed, and it was titled *Overcomer, Breaking Down the Walls of Shame and Rebuilding Your Soul.*

On top of the book was a card, and in it, my friend explained how excited she was that I was there and that she felt God had told her to give me this book. God also told her I had the gift of prophecy. I had no idea what the heck she was talking about as far as prophecy was concerned, but the book was amazing!

After we broke silence on the third day, we all gathered to eat lunch together and talk about what God did in our 48 hours and the things He spoke to us. My friend sits down at my table and says to me, "I know that God told me you have the gift of prophecy, you should write a book!"

Wait, excuse me? What did you just say? She never knew I wanted to write a book or that I even loved to write because I kept it a secret from most people, including her. I kept it a secret because that way, I wouldn't get hurt by people laughing or thinking it was crazy of me to write a book. I protected my dream out of the fear of rejection.

My friend never knew that I asked God to confirm to me if I should write a book during my silence. Through her, God was telling me to write. God also gave me the title for this book at that same retreat during my silence, even though I didn't know what I was going to write in the book until seven months later.

I already knew it wasn't "normal" to have to set yourself rules when it comes to writing. Not everyone likes to write so much that they can't allow themselves to write past 10:30 p.m. because they'll become so engulfed in what they're writing that they will stay up until 2 a.m. writing and only go to sleep not because they are yawning, oh no, you look past the yawning. It's because you know mid-day the next day, when the exhaustion sets in, you'll have all the regrets.

I even spoke to God recently and said, "Look, if this is going to be an actual thing you need me to do, can you please make it a day job, as in my full-time work during the day job because I'm getting really tired?"

My calling isn't being executed from all this free time that I have. I write when my daughter goes down to bed at night. I write when I don't feel like it, I write when I'm excited to write, and I write when I'm tired, stressed, and feeling compressed. I write after an eight-hour shift on my feet all day, and it's the most fulfilling part of my week, even through exhaustion.

What am I supposed to do, wait until I win the lottery, and then write? I've already asked God, it's not coming.

At that seven-month benchmark after my first silent retreat was when I attended an intensive. It was in beautiful Huntsville, Alabama. God spoke so many things to me on the fourth day of attending the intensive.

I was going through a divorce at the time and needed healing and confirmation on a multitude of things.

On the last day of the intensive, we gathered for worship and one last class before our goodbyes and fellowship. I walked out onto the deck of the enormous log cabin that we were so blessed to stay in, and I was explaining something that God had given me and confirmed for me when it came to my marriage to one of the leaders of the intensive. She began listening to me speak, and she was listening with such great intent that her eyes were closed so that she could *FEEL* what I was saying, and then bam, she stopped me mid-sentence and threw a title for a book at me.

I said, "Huh?" She repeated the title and then said, "It's a chapter in a book or the title of a book, and you've got to write it."

I looked at her with complete shock on my face because she, too, didn't know that I wrote or that I wanted to write books. She also didn't know that I asked God to confirm to me again by the time I left the intensive if I was called to write.

One month later, on a zoom call with the Kallah community, I was given a word by a woman leading the zoom, and she said to me, "Jaime, the word that I have for you is worthy; God says you are worthy and the Scripture I have for you is Ephesians 4:1."

I was like ok, that makes sense. I haven't felt worthy of prophet or pastor and all these gifts. I didn't feel worthy of writing either. I mean, this is a lot to take in.

But, what did Ephesians 4:1 (NLT) say? "Therefore I, a prisoner for serving the Lord, BEG YOU to lead a life WORTHY of your calling for you have been called by God".

I was like, dang, ok!

This is important stuff because when you see your Gifts of the Spirit or your five-fold, you may think you are not worthy of such a bold calling. Even if your calling looks different or you feel your calling is your kids and husband, then that too is beautiful and important and still requires you to use what God has given you.

A lot of people know who Joyce Meyer is, but not everyone knows her testimony. You can listen to her full testimony by just going to YouTube but also, she has a beautiful version called *Beauty for Ashes* that you can listen to on YouTube as well. In a very sad and disturbing short version of her testimony, her father forced her to have sex with him until she was eighteen years old.

But she went on to get married, had a baby, got divorced, and finally, she still found a man who loved her for her.

Her life was full of ups and down, and her healing didn't happen overnight. Unfortunately, I too, was sexually abused. I was twelve years old, and he was nineteen.

I have had so many hindrances in my life because of this one moment in my life, but thankfully, no more. But I remember hearing her testimony and then looking at my testimony and thinking, what do I have to complain about?

Then God so graciously spoke to me and said, "Let someone's testimony *HUMBLE* you, not *CRUMBLE* you." God was telling me that my hurts aren't irrelevant, and just because another person has been through more doesn't make mine less.

I can look at someone else's testimony and say, wow, that's incredible; I should be thankful that mine wasn't to the extent of hers. I should be thankful that mine was with a boy who was way too old for me and not my father. How horrific that must have been. Wow, how beautiful that she overcame that!

I have a lot to be thankful for because someone always has it worse. But that didn't mean I stuffed my pain inside. That doesn't mean I didn't need healing from my own incident. I think too often we do that, we let someone's story crumble us, and we stuff things down and never experience the humbling adventure of healing.

Your life isn't so far gone or too messed up for God to show up. There's a saying that says, "God already planned for your stupid." He already knew I would become pregnant at sixteen, He already knew that I would drop out of college many times. He knew I would be divorced three times and two of those to the same person, and many, many more wrong turns other than those.

He also knew that later I would give my life to Christ and learn about a Samaritan woman at a well who had been married five times and was living with a man who wasn't even her husband. Still, God would align her to meet up with Jesus at that well, and she would go on to have her own ministry spreading His Word.

He knew I would learn about a funny man named Moses who would ask God so many times, "Are you sure you called me?" That God would become angry and then, through grace, gift him his brother Aaron to speak for Moses because Moses was too insecure about his speech impediment.

He knew I would learn about Jonah high tailing it out of a boat to flee from what God wanted him to do and then spend some unwanted time in the belly of a fish only to be spat out into his calling.

He plans for our stupid, but who we are in Him has always been. He uses our lives and restores us, and it all works out for His glory.

Romans 8:28-30 (TPT) reads:

> "So we are convinced that every detail of our lives is continually woven together for good, for we are his lovers who have been called to fulfill his designed purpose. For he knew all about us before we were born, and he destined us from the beginning to share the likeness of his Son. This means the Son is the oldest among a cast family of brothers and sisters who will become just like him. Having determined our destiny ahead of time, he called us to himself and transferred his perfect righteousness to everyone he called. And those who possess his perfect righteousness he co-glorified with his Son!"

My testimony enhances my gifts to lead others, and so does yours! The Five-fold Ministry is a biblical outline we are gifted to equip people and grow in God's kingdom. We use the five-fold for our works of service. Knowing we are growing in Christ through supplying ourselves and the body of Christ will cause a mature blending of faith.

As you mature, you begin to grow in knowledge about God and His Word. You'll develop unwavering faith and experience His good and pleasing will for your life. You'll discover Him, worship Him and learn what it means to praise Him in every storm.

To the person reading this who just said, "Yeah, ok," with an eye roll. I hear you; I know that it seems easier said than done sometimes especially when He's quiet or seems far away, and you're filled with doubt. Remember who you are, and don't just read this because it sounded like something you should probably read but take what God has given you and *RUN* with it, be *ONE* with it.

DO THE WORK! Take the assessments I've placed in here because faith is an action word. Faith in Hebrew is; Emunah which means "to take firm action."

I can pray myself skinny, but until I put down the donut and pick up the apples, it's not happening. Could God do it for me? Well, absolutely, but will He? Nope, He won't because He's not a genie. He doesn't normally do what you *CAN* do, God is here to do what you *CAN'T* do.

You can dream about a promotion at work all day long and even hit all your numbers and be the best employee in the whole place, and God can put you in the position you prayed for, but if you let anxiety overtake you and turn it down, then that's on you.

Or you tell yourself that you aren't worthy of the promotion, and you don't take it because you lack the faith that gives you confidence. He's not going to snap His fingers and pop you into that position. He may continue to nudge you, but at the end of the day, you have to meet Him somewhere.

He gave us the power through faith to move that mountain from here to there, and it will move, and nothing will be impossible for you. (Matthew 17:20) But you have to move it.

It's not easy to move or to do things that God has called you to do. Joshua was given the commandment to be strong and courageous because he was terrified. Fear doesn't change your calling, but it will keep you from your calling.

Jonah was called on by God to go to Nineveh and prophesy disaster because of the city's immense sin. They say that today, it would be very similar to you being called on by God to walk up to an ISIS army as a believer and start preaching to them about the Word of God and how they are living in extreme sin.

H to the E to the double hockey sticks, NO! It's a one-way ticket to anywhere but there in a fish's belly for me. Yes, sir! He didn't say it would be easy, but He did say it would be worth it.

I had to learn as I went through the process of finding who I was in Christ that everything needed to be for Him. I knew I had to accept that even if this book was denied publishing, there was a purpose to writing it and that I was called to do it. If the calling was simply to write it so that I could better myself, then so be it, it would be hard to take in, but the blessings that flow from misunderstood obedience are extraordinary.

You don't have to understand everything, especially at that moment, to believe He is for you. It won't always feel like it in the moment, the days, the months, or even the years sometimes, but His timing isn't our timing.

So, go on and better yourself some more! Go to fivefoldministry.com and take an assessment, or I'll say it here and again later, you can also dive deeper by attending an Unveiling Intensive through Kallahculture.com.

After you take your Spiritual Gifts assessment and five-fold assessment, start to look over them daily. Pray that God speaks to you about the gifts and why He called you and gifted you these things. Look back over your life and see if you can remember glimpses of God showing you who you are through these gifts.

You may already be a teacher at a school and have always known what you wanted to do, and then you may have received Teacher as a gift, and that would make sense.

I remember asking my grandma if there was anything she ever wanted to do, and I asked her because she was an amputee. I wanted to know if she felt like she missed out on anything in that aspect. Secondly, I wanted to know because she was a wife and mom, and I always had this tugging at me beyond those things. She replied, "All I ever wanted to do was be a wife and a mother, and I did, so I'm happy."

It's beautiful being a wife and mother and it's one of the hardest jobs in the world. To know without a doubt that she wanted to do that and was content is perfect, and she was right where she needed to be. I can almost guarantee that my grandmother didn't know her Gifts of the Spirit, five-fold, strengths, and core values. Would she have sought more if she did? Maybe served in the church or held her own Bible studies in her home?

If you get something that doesn't make a whole lot of sense (and it should make some sense) but rather you don't fully understand why God has chosen these things for you, then that is perfectly normal. He will start to reveal things to you when you seek Him out. Focus on your top *TWO* five-folds.

Matthew 7:7-8 (TPT) says:

> "Ask, and the gift is yours. Seek, and you'll discover. Knock, and the door will be opened for you. For every persistent one will get what he asks for. Every persistent seeker will discover what he longs for. And everyone who knocks persistently will one day find a door."

List your top two Five-Fold Ministries (from fivefoldministry.
com) here:

1.
_____

2.
_____

Prayer

Father,

I thank you for the gifts given to me through grace and entrusted to me for glorifying your name. I ask for the opportunity to use, rely on, perfect, understand, and mature into my gifts. I am forever grateful for the time with you that allows me to strengthen who I was fearfully and wonderfully made to be. You are the lover of my soul, my rock, and my fortress.

In Jesus' Name, Amen

Chapter 5
Strengths

I think just about everyone can name at least one strength they may have. One strength about me that I've always known is that I can find laughter in just about any situation, and I love that about myself.

There's a country song about a woman who is having a really bad day, she gets into a car accident, and it happens to be her ex-boyfriend that she crashed into, and then as if that's not enough, she woke up late and is now late for work. But, in the chorus of the song, she says, "Let go laughing." I've always loved that, and it fits me perfectly, from the frantic running late morning to the let-go laughing.

That doesn't mean I let everything go laughing, but I am capable of laughing when the situation calls for my famous attitude of, "What else are you going to do?" But remember, sometimes our greatest strengths can be our biggest flaws.

I can also laugh at inappropriate times. I tend to make jokes and use sarcasm in moments that probably don't call for them. I can also sweep things under the rug and "laugh them off." I have a good sense of humor, but I can also have a dry sense of humor that causes people to not know if I'm joking or not. I'm apt to be the Simon and the Paula (Old person American Idol reference).

Part of knowing who you are is learning how you were designed and knowing how you tic, think, and learn and so on. Your strengths are how you grow, and it's a major part of how you function at work, why you get along with the people you do, have the friends you do, and it's also why you struggle in those same areas. The enemy will attack you where ever you are the most strong.

When you know your strengths;

- You get to have realistic expectations of yourself.
- You become attentive to where you are weak so that other people and the enemy can't attack you.
- By showcasing your unique self, you help other believers to walk in who they are.
- You can be free from striving for perfection to be like anyone else other than Jesus.
- Live realistically and be productive with your weaknesses, knowing you are flawed, but nothing is mistaken about you.
- Always be working to build up your strengths and lower your weaknesses.

I'm going to share and dive into my strengths and then my weaknesses that go hand in hand with my strengths. Please know that self-discovery is an ongoing process. Sometimes you go through seasons where you need to be a certain way to get through the day. Like being at a job that you don't like, but it pays the bills. Maybe while at that job, you're putting a smile on your face so hard that you're pretty sure it might be causing some wrinkles, and you're trying to just get through the day as the light in the darkness. That job is possibly bringing out more of your weaknesses, and it's an opportunity to learn to use your strengths better in work situations.

Unfortunately, I had a situation at a job where I went to someone and tried to explain what had happened or what I felt was my perspective in that certain situation.

This was a customer service job and it had happened in other scenarios, it was important to talk about the situation that had occurred so that we could be on the same page and grow from it.

As I began to explain myself during a mutual open conversation, my co-worker began talking over me. So, I began explaining myself again after letting the co-worker know she wasn't listening. Well, I was reminded really quickly that I do not like when people talk over me as she began to speak over me yet again.

I began to get upset and could feel that very soon, I wouldn't be handling the situation right either. Then one word led to another, and before I knew it, the both of us were indeed not listening, and miscommunication was flying everywhere, causing me to lash out. I said a four-letter word that shouldn't be said and especially at work.

After a day or so had passed, I spoke with God, and I said, "I don't ever want to do that again; help me and remind me with a word that will calm me and help me adjust my helmet of salvation when I'm in situations like this." The Lord responded with, "*CAPTIVE*", I was to hold my mouth, emotions, and thoughts captive in moments of anger, especially those moments when you feel like you're about to lose control.

There have been times since that day that I have had to be reminded of the word captive, and it's worked. There have been situations when I haven't responded correctly but when remembering the code word, I was able to reel myself in. The Lord will lead you when you ask Him. It's ok to weed your garden every day, go to God to help you walk in the fruit of the spirit and suit up in your armor for the day.

My first strength is ***individualization***. Individualization is when I can see the uniqueness in all individuals, I can sense that "one size doesn't fit all," and appreciate the differences in others. I love to hear other people's perspectives; I love when people are different, and I especially love when I can get along with those who are different from me because I tend to use it as an opportunity to learn. All three of my children are different, and I love it.

The weakness that can come from individualization, if I do not learn who I am or if I let the enemy get to me is that I can become unable to combine myself with groups of people because I tend to be shy and or the unusual, awkward one in the group. I'm likely to offer up taking the group project home and doing it myself and then just adding everyone's name to it.

My next strength is *input;* I can be a great resource or someone you would want to come and talk to about things. I can be knowledgeable and have an excellent memory.

I've been a hairstylist for fifteen years, and I never understood why I could cut someone's hair one time and not see them for ten weeks and then, after two minutes of talking with them, have a piece of our conversation from ten weeks ago pop into my head like, "Oh, yeah how is your puppy Cooper and your new job you were about to start?" They literally look at me like I've been stalking them.

The funny thing is that I have no idea what I ate for breakfast that morning, but I can assure you I know what restaurant a random Tom was taking his wife to eight weeks ago.

Of course, everything is for God's glory, right? So, I know now that it's a trait that God uses as I combine individualization and input. I didn't pick those, it's just how God made me but how cool that I can see the difference in people and then remember little details about them to make them feel special! And, even though they think I'm a stalker, it does bring a smile to their face. Other traits for input are to have attention to detail.

The weakness for input is that I can know a lot of useless information. I tend to like to know things, and that will be better explained in my next strength, but sometimes I'm astonished by how I knew something or why I felt the need to learn or know it. I can also lack focus and I can be notorious for starting something and stopping it (Just don't ask me how my diet is going).

I can be a boring conversationalist rambling on about nothing. I tend to trail off and think of clowns riding elephants if the other person's conversation is boring or if I'm not interested in it or, most likely, I have a lot on my mind. However, 90% of the problem is contributed to my short attention span, it's similar to that of a four-year-old.

This leads me to the last weakness, and that is a cluttered mind. If I'm not careful, then there's also a cluttered home, but interestingly enough, I have the opposite side of me who often cleans, freaks out about every six months or so, and throws everything in my line of fire away.

Learner is my next strength; I'm always willing to learn even if I don't like it and usually catch on quickly (just keep me away from technology). I tend to be interested in many different things and find life and other cultures intriguing.

My weakness for this strength is that I can apparently be a know-it-all. My ex-husband got me a tee shirt that read, "I'm not arguing, I'm just explaining why I'm right." He possesses the same "quality" which would explain why we loved to go head to head to acknowledge our knowledge.

My next weakness can be bookish, in other words, I would rather read and study a book rather than learn about worldly interests. There could be robotic frogs going around assaulting people with mini knives, and I wouldn't know because I don't watch the news or turn anything on that would tell me about it.

I have to force myself to know even the simplest glimpse of politics. I would rather sit at home and write a book than socialize. Did you ever see the meme that said, "You better invite me, I'm not coming, but I still want to be included?" Well, that's me, except for when I do want to socialize but not for too long, no ma'am, just enough socializing so that I can get back home in time, to be home, for no reason.

Intellection is my next strength, and I can be an excellent thinker, a lot of who I am, comes down to being a thinker, if you haven't noticed. My mind is creative, which I have mentioned before. It's caused me to write this book, it's caused sleeping issues and, if I'm not careful, anxiety. It can cause me to forget what I'm saying mid-sentence or be extremely detailed.

I can enjoy musing and I believe that it's good to stop and smell the roses. I have a very laid-back side to me, and being able to work alone is another addition to intellection. I can also think deeply and I love that because not everyone can.

For instance, have you ever poured your heart out to someone who acted like they wanted to hear what was bothering or stressing you out? But they couldn't respond well because they didn't think deeply, so they responded with something super simple like, "Wow, well, good luck to you." They don't have it in their DNA to give a detailed, compassionate response or to go back and forth with the conversation. Which is fine, that's how God made them.

My weakness for intellection, even though I've already mentioned a few, is that I can be a loner; I can be a homebody for sure. I definitely socialized a lot more when I was younger, but my life has changed. My social circle, goals, morals, and values are all different, and that can weed out and redirect your life. I realized I just seem to be a little different from everyone else. At least it feels like that.

I remember watching SNL one time years ago and thinking, "*Those are my people.*" Not the lifestyle they live but the comedic tendency and weirdness to them. I can also be slow to act or waste time thinking *TOO* much.

Do you ever start thinking about something and then realize 20 minutes has gone bye and you have day-dreamed an entire scenario that is never going to happen or is so off the wall that you have to immediately rebuke it in Jesus' name? Maybe you've even started crying based on this scenario and got yourself all worked up just to wipe your tears away and say to yourself, *"What in the world of all things hideous was that?"* I blame it on all the horror movies I watched before Jesus entered my life.

Last but not least, because this is just my top five, is **empathy.** I create trust, and I'm a loyal person, I would rather have a few friends instead of a bunch of friends just to have them. I bring healing to those who get to know me and allow myself to know them by listening and pouring into them. I can customize my approach to each person, which I love because, as you read above in individualization, I love to know someone as an individual. It will help you to know how to approach that person and speak life into them. Not everyone benefits from the same approach.

I can also be too sensitive, and carry the weight of other people's stress on my shoulders. Which can be emotionally and sometimes mentally exhausting when pairing empathy with my Spiritual Gifts of mercy, prophecy, and discernment because I'm all in my feelings and thinking so much that if I'm not careful, I can become over stimulated and crash being impatient and short with those around me.

Whew, that's just my top five. I'm exhausted with myself and all of my flawed greatness. I never knew how to dive into who I was or why I thought the way I did, or even how I did the things I did and still do. I cannot express how good it feels to know who I am as an individual child of God.

I love how the results of who I am stand alone but also intertwine with each other so that it all fits and makes sense.

I always asked God why He made me the way He did, but I never understood. I thought He had made a mistake. But guess what? God doesn't make mistakes. We misunderstand. In the mess of my confusion, God was always there and knew just how He made me.

It's not like when you bake a batch of cookies, and then you taste them and realize something went wrong. God doesn't look back over you like a bad batch of cookies and go, "Oops-a-daisy, too much salt on that one." And then toss you out and start over. He perfects you with faith that builds endurance and confidence that wills you to live more righteous in your relationship with Him.

I finally got my answer at my silent retreat after years of asking, "God, why did you make me this way? I feel like so many different things, and I just can't figure out who I am?" His reply was, "Because I made you like a coat of many colors." I can't even type that without smiling.

I would be lying if I said that hearing that didn't make me want to immediately go buy a coat with many colors and strut around like a psychopath, just smiling and waving anywhere and everywhere for no reason other than to just show off how proud I felt wearing who I was in the sight of God.

I'm a stained-glass window that's beautiful when the sun is down, and my season looks dark but immense with character when the SON shines through, projecting a variety of colors that help in God's kingdom in all sorts of ways.

One morning, I peered out the window on my silent retreat and noticed that these trees were warped after it had rained. They just hung over at the top as though they were sad and droopy. God said to me, "Even a tree hangs over when it's rained on but springs back to life when the sun comes out." That tree stood tall, it didn't fall over with the heaviness of the rain but carried the weight of it until it healed from it.

I've been rained on, and I've felt sad and warped. I know it feels like you've been poured on, but God says in Titus 3:6 (NLT). "He generously POURED out the Spirit upon us through Jesus Christ our Savior".

You are not hopeless, you just need a new perspective. You can be poured on by the love of Jesus, or you can let life pour on you.

If you would like to find out your strengths, just go to Gallup. com, and there you can take your CliftonStrenghts assessment. I took the smallest test that will focus on your top five. Dive into them, and as you read them, pray for God to show you things about yourself that correlate with the answers you received, and then journal about who you are and why these are your strengths.

List your top five CliftonStrengths here:

1.
_____

2.
_____

3.
_____

4.
_____

5.
_____

Prayer

Jesus,
I love you and I love the way you love me. I have strength because you alone give me strength. Thank you for guiding me through my strengths and weaknesses. Teach me when to be strong and when to be alert to the enemy and his lies.
In Jesus name, Amen.

CHAPTER 6

Core Values

As much as I would love to consider chewing with your mouth shut and not exploiting innocent bystanders to your mouth noises as my number one core value (It's called Misophonia, and it's an actual phobia) it's not the kind of core value I'm speaking of.

Core values represent how you prioritize your life, they represent why you care so deeply about the things you do. They should be a driving force in how you display your representation of Jesus. Your belief system should be behind your core values.

I used to think that core values were things like, being nice, not hitting people (that's frowned upon, by the way), not murdering (also frowned upon), table manners, you know, stuff like that, and all the Ten Commandments. However, it's deeper than that.

One of my core values is *honesty*. Obviously, we all value honesty on some level, but I can assure you that not all people hold that value to the same level. I've learned that honesty is something that can cause me to just tell someone something in a straightforward manner. One of my sisters always says she knows that if she wants an honest answer about something, she'll ask me. So, while sometimes it can be offensive, it can also be something about me that other people value.

I also appreciate honesty from other people. I don't always love to hear honesty or even at times respond well to the honesty at first but if it's coming from someone that I respect and know has my best interest at heart, I can think about the honest advice and appreciate it.

God is honest, I don't always like what God is telling me, but I can assure you I appreciate it and value it.

Focus is hilarious as a core value coming from me after I just explained how I can have a wandering mind. But focus is very important to me, writing this book takes a lot of focus.

When I'm at work, I can get in the zone. We can get busy, and it's just a go, go, go environment. If that focus is interrupted, it becomes frustrating to me. And because I'm such a thinker, I can become set on certain plans. For instance, if I get my mind set on something, I begin to create, imagine and focus on that thing. If the plan falls through or if you change course, it can be frustrating or disappointing because now my brain has to shift.

So, while I can have a mind that is easily distracted, I can also have a mind that thrives on focus to survive and keep me going.

Courage and *strength* are two more of my core values. I absolutely love these two because not only did He command us to be strong and courageous (Joshua 1:9), but I can look back over my life and see moments and seasons when I had to be strong and courageous. I know for a fact that you've had to be strong and courageous and probably more than I have ever had to be. People go through some extraordinary things in life.

All of our core values come from God, we thrive through Jesus. But, sometimes, we fall short of our values. We may be in a toxic relationship that doesn't allow us to live to our full potential. We may be stressed at work, and maybe God is calling us into something else that will take a lot of strength and courage to believe in. Did you know that strength is the definition of courage? Courage is *strength* in the face of pain, fear, or grief.

God didn't just tell Joshua to be courageous, He didn't just tell him to be strong. He said, be strong AND courageous! It takes strength, which is something that can withstand great force or pressure to be courageous in the face of pain, fear, or grief.

Balance is the next core value that I have, and nothing is more annoying than being out of balance. Hormones will do it, that's for sure, and that's hard enough, then you add on work, family, and our minds being out of balance, which can complicate life.

1 Corinthians 12:21-26 (TPT) reads,

> "It would be wrong for the eye to say to the hand, "I don't need you," and equally wrong if the head said to the foot, "I don't need you." In fact, the weaker our parts, the more vital and essential they are."

This is balance. It goes on to say that he has mingled the body parts together. It says it gives higher honor to the lesser parts and that "He has done this intentionally so that EVERY MEMBER WOULD LOOK AFTER THE OTHERS with mutual concern, and so that there will be no division in the body." 1 Corinthians 12:25 (TPT).

That Scripture is balance. He literally gave me my gifts, values, talents, strengths, and five-folds so that I can look after (balance out) and assist my sisters and brothers in Christ who have different gifts, values, talents, strengths, and five-folds than me. He created me just how He needed me to be, so that I could guide others in the way He needs me too.

I met someone who had the gift of craftsmanship. She could draw and sketch very beautifully, and when she got a word from God, she would receive an image in her mind and then sketch a bird or flower or whatever it was, which would turn out incredible. It was unique and beautiful to watch.

Listen, If God wanted a word delivered through doodling and stick people, He would choose me. But it's not likely, so I'll stay in my lane.

Proverbs 11:1 (ESV) says, "A false balance is an abomination to the Lord, but a just weight is his delight."

Well, hello, balance. Don't force yourself to lead a life that God never intended for you. I've started and stopped so many different things trying to find my place and be successful at things I watched my friends doing.

I remember God showing me a vision of a basketball court with cracks in it. The cracks had weeds growing out of them and there was no one to be found and not one set of bleachers filled with spectators cheering me on. It was deserted.

I said to God, "I don't play sports, why are you showing me this?" He responded with, "Stop trying to play a game I never intended for you to play." Even God wasn't coming to watch my game.

I know you think that it feels impossible to get balance in your life. I'm sitting here at my great grandmother's desk (who also wrote a book interestingly enough, I wonder if she wrote it at this very desk) in my small two-bedroom apartment that I got after my divorce, where I sleep on the couch so that my two kids can have their own bedrooms. I'm trying to figure out inflation and gas prices and time with each of my children. I miss them as I send them off, and I sometimes go into their rooms and just snuggle their blankets because it's like a part of me is gone when they are away, and yet this is the most balanced I have felt in my whole life.

Before you think I'm nuts for feeling balanced in a transition period that feels vast with unknown questions, unanswered prayers and a sprinkle of loneliness and grief, let me just tell you that knowing who I am and creating a relationship with God has been one of the most balancing things I have ever done and nothing I go through will shake my faith because of it.

I sat here not long after I moved in, and I began to just have a pity party. I was thinking about how I wanted more, how I was frustrated that every other more updated apartment that became available, God took away. No washer and dryer, no dishwasher, and no third bedroom for me, and to make matters worse, *Bill and Ted's Excellent Adventure, Wayne's World, Dude Where's My Car*, moves in next door to me and plays loud music. The guy above me has an old recliner, and I know that only because I can hear it every time he slams it shut.

God immediately shut the pity party down by saying, "Oh, but Paul wrote for me in a jail cell, so how blessed are you?" Does God ever say something to you and you just kind of look around for a minute? Not with your head, just your eyes move back and forth like, dang it, that was really good, and I can't even argue with that.

God has things for you to do, whether you have a mansion or a two-bedroom apartment in a small town, and He will humble you quickly. I'm not writing this on a fancy computer with the newest and greatest author softer ware. No, this is being brought to you by Word 2003 with what I call "the tank," and that would be my old computer. Those more updated apartments or the three-bedroom apartments were more expensive, God defiantly kept taking them away from me.

In addition to all of that, I planned on having my car for another one to two years. My car had other plans, and I had to get a new one. With a new car comes a car payment, so God knew better than I did, and I'm grateful for His love.

God will balance out every part of your life, even when you think it's falling apart, He's preparing a comeback.

Peace is knowing that God is with you. Peace can be the goose bumps that run down your spine when the Holy Spirit is present. Peace is the smile on your face when God gives you a word. Peace is a deep breath when you accept that everything is going to be okay.

Peace is one of my core values, and it's the sweetest of them all. When we have a relationship with Him, and we pray and give thanks for everything, then we can have the PEACE that surpasses all understanding which will guard our heart and mind in Christ Jesus.

Can I just say that even in moments when I don't feel peace, which can sometimes be often, especially if I'm driving, that worship music or prayer can lift me away from the anxiety and remind me to calm down and guard my heart and my mind.

When you feel peace, you feel relaxed, and when you're making the right decision, you need peace. Peace is an important feeling and presence to encounter and include in your life.

Last but not least for me is *Joy*. Joy, along with peace, is part of walking in the fruit of the spirit, it's knowing that my Joy comes from who we are in Christ and not who we are through work, a spouse, and definitely not through our angry teenager's eyes. We don't constantly feel joy in everything, but we can rest assured that joy is hidden even in the darkest seasons.

I happen to be having a hard time this week being away from my daughter. If I'm not careful, it can give me anxiety, but while I can keep the anxiety at bay through prayer, I do find myself feeling sad when I see her empty room or don't get to climb into her bed in the morning and see how excited she is to be awake and see me. I'm not robbed of joy in the sense that it's just gone completely, but I am feeling sad for a moment, and that's ok. It's not the feeling sad that's the problem, it's if I was to stay sad and feed off it.

Joy is important to me because I think it's important to find joy each day. Pastors did a trend a few years back where they would preach about how the Bible doesn't use the word happy. They would speak about how we are not promised to be happy and to stop using the word happy when it pertains to God because He said you would have trials and tribulations and blah, blah, blah.

Yep, I get what they are saying, at the end of the day, what they are getting at is not wrong. They would go on to say in their sermons that the actual word "happy" isn't in the Bible. My thought is that plenty of other words don't translate to the English language either.

But, do you know what word the Bible does have? Joy! Joy seems pretty happy to me. Joy is a feeling of great pleasure or happiness. God doesn't promise us a life without trials, but He does say that joy is something we can have and walk in, and for us, that translates to happiness.

My kids' laughing brings happiness, joy, and peace, it's all of the words, and in the Bible, the name Isaac means "the one who laughs" because God is good, and He knows that laughter brightens us. Jesus felt happiness, Jesus laughed, and a chemical shift happens in our brains when we laugh. I'm sure Mary felt joy and happiness when she looked at baby Jesus.

Have you ever laughed super hard, I mean belly laughed, and then said with a deep breath, "I needed that?" It's because you did, and God created you to need it.

FINDING YOUR CORE VALUES

I'm going to guide you through finding your core values by breaking down each section with the 8x4x2x1 method. ***Make sure you pray and ask the Holy Spirit to guide you to each core value!***

You'll see eight Core Values listed in each set. In Round 1, pick four from the eight listed by writing out the CORE VALUE and NOT THE NUMBER. It's easier to decide which value God is leading you towards when you can see them in each round by writing them out.

Next, go to round 2 and pick two core values from round 1.

Then pick one core value from round 2 as your final Core Value writing it out at the bottom of each set of eight until you reach your seven Core Values.

Here's a random example:

CORE VALUES	ROUND 1	ROUND 2
1. Accuracy		
2. Achievement	1. Accuracy	
3. Authenticity		
4. Balance	2. Balance	1. Balance
5. Boldness		
6. Consistency	3. Boldness	2. Compassion
7. Compassion		
8. Confidence	4. Compassion	

CORE VALUE #1 Balance

NOW IT'S YOUR TURN!

CORE VALUES	ROUND 1	ROUND 2
1. Accuracy		
2. Achievement	1._____	
3. Authenticity		
4. Balance	2._____	1._____
5. Boldness		
6. Consistency	3._____	2._____
7. Compassion		
8. Confidence	4._____	

CORE VALUE #1_____

CORE VALUES	ROUND 1	ROUND 2
1. Creativity		
2. Commitment	1._____	
3. Charity		
4. Communication	2._____	1._____
5. Caring		
6. Courage	3._____	2._____
7. Calmness		
8. Dependable	4._____	

CORE VALUE #2_____

CORE VALUES	ROUND 1	ROUND 2
1. Determination		
2. Decisiveness	1._____	
3. Disciplined		
4. Excellence	2._____	1._____
5. Efficiency		
6. Faithfulness	3._____	2._____
7. Focus		
8. Flexibility	4._____	

CORE VALUE #3_____

CORE VALUES	ROUND 1	ROUND 2
1. Growth		
2. Goodness	1._____	
3. Generosity		
4. Grace	2._____	1._____
5. Gratitude		
6. Honesty	3._____	2._____
7. Honor		
8. Humility	4._____	

CORE VALUE #4_____

CORE VALUES	ROUND 1	ROUND 2
1. Inspire		
2. Integrity	1._____	
3. Joy		
4. Justice	2._____	1._____
5. Kindness		
6. Loyalty	3._____	2._____
7. Love		
8. Obedience	4._____	

CORE VALUE #5_____

CORE VALUES	ROUND 1	ROUND 2
1. Organization		
2. Peace	1._____	
3. Passion		
4. Patience	2._____	1._____
5. Positive		
6. Perseverance	3._____	2._____
7. Quality		
8. Respect	4._____	

CORE VALUE #6_____

CORE VALUES	ROUND 1	ROUND 2
1. Resilience		
2. Relationships	1._____	
3. Strength		
4. Self- control	2._____	1._____
5. Teachable		
6. Trustworthy	3._____	2._____
7. Vulnerability		
8. Wholeness	4._____	

CORE VALUE #7_____

Write out all of your Core Values here;

1._____
2._____
3._____
4._____
5._____
6._____
7._____

These are your seven Core Values which you will use to operate and guide you in life. Make sure you go before God and examine each one asking Him to reveal why He made you with those core values and write down what He tells you. If you have a moment in life that makes you realize why you possess one of your core values, then write that moment down. It could be a rule in your home or something that comforts you.

Maybe one of your core values is respect, and you have a lot of rules in your life about respect and just didn't realize it was your core value. Dig into that and find out where it came from. Remember, you're on a journey to get to know yourself, and writing these things down and reviewing them will help you better understand yourself.

You might take this again six months from now and get a different core value. It's highly unlikely God would have you change all seven considering this is how He made you to operate. But seasons change and look different. Coming out of a divorce has led me to have different core values than I may have had two years ago. I can assure you I don't have all the same core values now that I did before I was a believer.

Maybe you take this while you're pregnant, and then in 10 months after you've spent some time as a new mom, God gives you a new core value. As I said, the meat and potatoes of your core values will probably stand firm, but as seasons shift and sway, so can the way you view life and your needs in life.

You could also sit down as a family and go over each round, deciding what your core values are for your home as a group of people who have to co-exist together. Or what are your core values as a parent? It's a valuable tool to help you discover how to walk through life.

Some of the core values of just being a follower of Christ are love, compassion, and respect. When we love, we think about others (and it's our second greatest commandment). When we have compassion, we can picture being in someone else's shoes, and when we respect, we can value people even though we have differences.

You may not be the greatest at all of these and need to work on it, and that's ok. I work in customer service, so I can assure you that I'm tested constantly, and while most days I have patience, sometimes I forget to respond with love which covers a multitude of Karen's. sins, I meant to say sins. (1 Peter 4:8)

My middle son's best friend has a similar but yet huge difference in his choice of religion than we do. Meaning some of it has the same belief system as us, but there are additions to it that we don't believe in our home according to how we view the Bible. I can ask his friend's mom questions, and she can ask me questions. We respectfully answer and listen. I didn't want my son to attend any of the Bible studies that his friend goes to because we do not believe all of the same things, and his friend's mother received it with respect, grace, honor, compassion, and love.

I think we need more of that in the world. We should listen to each other more. If you notice, whenever Jesus was confronted about what He was teaching, He was able to respond boldly but not rudely. He didn't ignore them or scream at them but rather tried to educate them and conversed with people who believed He wasn't the Messiah and who believed He was doing everything wrong.

In the book of Mark, Jesus was confronted about working on the Sabbath because His disciples were eating the wheat (can you imagine that being a snack while you walked everywhere? No granola bar or trail mix stashed in anyone's satchel, no sir, just some wheat straight up from the wheat field, delish).

Mark 3:5 (NLT) says, "He looked around at them ANGRILY and was deeply saddened by their hard hearts."

I can just envision Jesus taking a deep sigh while His heart starts racing from anger. I mean, how many times does Jesus have to defend Himself? It had to be maddening. It goes on to say, "Then he said to the man, 'hold out your hand.' So the man held out his hand, and it was restored!"

Jesus responded with love by healing a man's infirmity after He was angry, annoyed, and deeply saddened. Then, after Jesus healed this man, the Pharisees ran away and plotted how to kill Jesus.

We've all been in situations where we have blessed someone and then been betrayed. Being married is full of blessings and disappointments. Being a parent is full of blessings and disappointments (especially with teenagers). But it didn't stop Jesus from teaching. It didn't stop Jesus from blessing, and it didn't stop His emotions, he was still saddened and probably still angry at them as they walked away, and He knew exactly what they were running away to do.

1 Peter 3:9-12 (NLT) reads:

> "Don't repay evil for evil. Don't retaliate with insults when people insult you. Instead, pay them back with a blessing. That is what God has CALLED you to do, and he will grant you his blessing." For the Scriptures say, "If you want to enjoy life and

see many HAPPY days, keep your tongue from speaking evil and your lips from telling lies. Turn away from evil and do good. Search for peace, and WORK TO MAINTAIN IT. The eyes of the Lord watch over those who do right, and his ears are open to their prayers. But the Lord turns his face against those who do evil."

It says, "Work to maintain it" we have to work at having peace, and it doesn't always come naturally because we were made to have emotions and God considers retaliating as evil. But, we have access to peace and joy because we have the fruit of the spirit in abundance. We just have to tap into it. If having a clean house brings you peace, then clean it. What does the fruit of the spirit look like? How do you obtain it?

I've been evil a time or two in my life according to the Scripture above. Has someone ever said something to you, and then your blood immediately started to boil because you're about to go into protection mode? Protecting your faith, yourself, your spouse, or your child because essentially that's all anger really is, is protection. But we are *CALLED* to protect with a *BLESSING*. Does that mean that if someone punches you in the face, you defend yourself by hugging the aggressor? No, probably not. It would be an interesting sight, though.

So, I'll say it again and again, it's easier said than done, but if we "weed" it every day and if we learn each other and ourselves, then blessing's come from it.

I give teenagers a bad wrap, but I have learned so much from being a mom to teenagers.

I tell my oldest son that your first child is like a pancake, you tend to burn the first one. This always ends with me laughing and him rolling his eyes and trying not to laugh at mom's joke that he's heard one million times. What it really means is that I missed the mark a lot when it came to my first son but through that experience I can be better and use it for my other children.

One thing I've learned about my second son is that he and I have to ask each other questions. For instance, remember when I said I have a dry sense of humor? Well, sometimes when I scold my son, he will smirk at me, making me feel disrespected, and then I start to get after him about how he needs to wipe that smirk off his face and so on.   I'm not living like Jesus in the angry moment, and what my son revealed to me after we sat down and talked was that he doesn't know if I'm joking or not, so he's smirking as if I'm joking with him. But he can't tell me at that moment because he's the type of person to shut down or just take what's being dished out to him even if he doesn't agree. After all, it's pressure or stress, and he doesn't do well with either.

So, to make our communication better, I had to give him permission to ask me at that moment, "Mom, are you being serious right now because I can't tell." Then I have to respond with a yes or a no because I made that a safe moment for him to ask me that question.

Sometimes I can be irritable and be impatient, and it just so happened that my middle son was nicknamed sloth. The kid has two modes; slow and slower. As I said, he doesn't do well under pressure, so I had to give my son permission to say to me, "Mom, can you please have patience with me right now." It immediately helps me to stop and recognize what I'm doing. It also teaches him to be an advocate for himself instead of just holding things in.

I had to explain to him that yes, we pick on him about being a sloth just like I'm picked on for being in outer space all the time, but I also make sure to tell him that God made him that way. He made him to be laid back and easy-going, and I love that about him.

I want to pull my hair out sometimes because of it, but at the end of the day, I think it's the coolest thing ever.

So, straighten your crown because it's going to get crooked sometimes. You're going to have people, moments, and situations that try to knock it right off of your head, but you have values and morals that align with your creator. You are a princess, the daughter of a king!

Prayer

Father,
Help me to place value in my self and in all the wonderful things that you need me to do. Help bring light to heavenly morals that I can display for your glory. Shift my heart from a heart of stone to a heart of flesh that I can place in your hands. Bring every thought captive to release new meaning in my life.
In Jesus name, Amen

CHAPTER 7
Emet!

Well, it's here, the extended version of oppression that I promised you. Emet is the Hebrew word for truth and not just half-truth or a little bit of the truth, but emet means the whole truth, and the truth is that we can be oppressed by unclean spirits. Truth is important to set you free, and when you're set free, you strengthen your ability to listen!

This chapter will contain a few more things beyond oppression like; strongholds and trauma. It's important to go over what could be hindering your full potential and your all-embracing freedom.

Remember the basic meaning of oppression is to crush or burden by abuse of power. The enemy is the king of oppression. He enjoys it, and unfortunately, he's good at it. He shows up in our homes and turns us against each other. He lurks at work, he provides tempers to those who are weak to stress, and he causes turmoil in any area he can.

There's a scene in one of the Wonder Woman movies where she's fighting so fast that they slow down the movie so you can get a feel for the speed and cunningness of the fight. In one particular moment, they do this with one of the evil characters making it seem as if he's quickly moving from one person to the next. The bad guy comes behind people and whispers in their ears, and then they immediately act on what he's telling them to do. I couldn't help but think it was the perfect visual of what's happening in the spirit realm when warfare is present in your life. The enemy and his army are penetrating your thoughts with whispers of offense and anything else that he knows will ruffle your feathers.

During an experiential prayer, God gave me a vision, and towards the end of that vision, I was standing on top of a cliff with Jesus. We were holding hands, and at this point in the vision, He was older with white hair and He was wearing a white robe. I think He may have represented His oneness with God at this particular scene in my mind. I would later go on to learn that Jesus is depicted as having white hair as well as wearing a white robe in Revelations 1:14-15. I had no knowledge of that prior to the vision.

Jesus and I were smiling at each other, and the presence I felt was peaceful and calm. At the bottom of the cliff was a beach, and I got the perception that the water before us was the ocean. I knew we had to get down from the cliff, so I turned to Jesus, and I asked Him how to get down. He said, "We jump." He was telling me to trust Him and have faith that He will always be with me.

Interestingly enough, Satan brought Jesus to a cliff or, as the Bible says, a super-duper high mountain.

Matthew 4:8-10 (TPT) reads:

> "And the third time the accuser lifted Jesus up onto a very high mountain range and showed him all the kingdoms of the world and all the splendor that goes with it." "All of these kingdoms I will give to you," the accuser said, "If only you will kneel down before me and worship me." But Jesus said, "Go away, Satan! For the Scriptures say: Kneel before the Lord your God and worship only him."

It says, "The third time," which means if you read above this Scripture, He had already been tested twice before Satan brought Jesus to the mountain. Jesus had been out in the wilderness, fasting and praying for 40 days and 40 nights. I fasted from coffee once, and I'm pretty sure I lost sight in my right ear. Yes, I know I wrote ear, that's how terrible it was! I repeat, Jesus fasted for 40 days and 40 nights! I bet His body was weak, but His commitment was still strong.

Satan knows what he's doing. First, he tempted Jesus with bread, yes, bread. Not kale, but carbs. Satan knows exactly what we *DON'T* need and wants to hand-feed it to us with his army, who lurks around studying you.

How arrogant do you have to be to offer the son of God all the kingdoms, amongst other things, and quote Scripture? Jesus said get behind me, Satan. He had the authority to make him leave, and it blows my mind that Satan tried to hand-feed Jesus some manipulation even though Jesus had authority. That alone should be a light bulb that even a believer needs to be on their game because Satan will try to serve you a dish, and it's your choice to eat it or deny it. Satan is the creator of reverse psychology. He used it to trick Eve in the garden, and he tried using it on Jesus.

In addition to that, I read this Scripture and can't help but notice a similarity in my vision that there was a high mountain or cliff and that Jesus, too, was taken to a high mountain. I got the feeling that God was telling me to be vigilant.

He was reminding me that Satan is always neck and neck with what God is trying to do. God will prevail, but if you are not careful, the confusion, oh my goodness, the confusion that can occur, is powerful. You can be on top with God, or you can be on top with the enemy. Free will is a powerful thing. The choice is always ours.

Jesus had a choice at that moment. All He had to do was either say yes to Satan or tell him to go away.

That doesn't mean that we blame everything on the devil. If God has been speaking to you about getting your breaks replaced but you keep putting it off and end up in an accident because your breaks went out, then who's to blame? The devil didn't do it!

Now, could the enemy use that moment as a feast to penetrate your thoughts and stack up the negative images and what-ifs that could have occurred from that incident? Yes, but the initial cause of the incident was your lack, not the enemies. Nor was it God's fault.

Is it me picking up the donuts, or is it the enemy? Well, that depends on your relationship with food, is a donut something you have multiple times a day or even a week, or is it something on occasion? Is it you, or is it a spirit of gluttony?

This is why reading Scripture and having a relationship with God is important so that you can catch yourself doing these things and correct or cast them away. We also have to want it to go away and believe it's done. I've rebuked chocolate multiple times, but it still appears so, there's that. Clearly, I don't want it gone bad enough.

Made To Crave is an amazing book written by Lysa Terkeurst, and I remember reading about how she had to put a Bible in her pantry to remind her that she could overcome anything in that pantry through Christ who strengthens her.

Is junk food hindering your life? Do you feel sluggish, unhappy, and have a foggy mind? I know I do when I don't eat right. Do you have an addiction to alcohol, drugs, sex, or pornography? I know how that goes because I used to have an addiction to pornography. I realize it's not the norm for a woman, but I was sexually abused, and nobody could hurt me through a screen. So, I felt safe being sexually free during moments with pornography. Is it something I looked at every day? No. It doesn't matter if it was just a couple of times a month, the condemnation I felt mixed with guilt and the inability to deny the urge to look at it when the thought came to mind made it an addiction. I refuse to outcast myself as someone who didn't have an issue just because it wasn't as frequent as most people. That would make me a hypocrite.

I've been blessed to be free from that addiction for five years now but do you think that the enemy doesn't try to tempt me? Remember, Jesus was offered bread while fasting from food. While sugar and chocolate do appear in my home, and a sugar fast is something I would greatly benefit from, pornography will never appear in my home again. That is the difference between *WISHING* to be free from something and *WANTING* to be free from it.

It was an addiction that came from someone else's free will to choose to take my innocence, and while pornography wasn't something I was proud of, I can recognize that it was a defense mechanism to my pain.

The Holy Spirit is here to help us, not just be around us but within us.

2 Corinthians 4:16 (NLT) "That is why we never give up. Though our bodies are dying, our spirits are being renewed every day."

I absolutely love this "being renewed every day." We need help, and we need to know that in a life of overflowing circumstances, we need pruning. The enemy might back off for a while, but he always returns.

In the Bible, the Hebrew word for "covenant" is *berith,* the root meaning "cut." Any kind of covenant in the Bible is linked to a blood sacrifice. Blood flows through the heart and races if we are upset, mad, or even exercising, and we have the ability to use our minds to calm the heart down and lower the blood pressure and heart rate.

On the cross, they used a hyssop branch to dip in the gall (a NOT so very top shelf wine with a large hint of vinegar or what some believe to be a slightly poisonous way to help with discomfort) and offer it to Jesus. The hyssop branch was known to be used to soak up blood after a sacrifice. Jesus refused the gall. He wasn't interested in numbing His pain. Because of His sacrifice on the cross, we no longer have to give a blood sacrifice, but how interesting that we still have the ability to use fasting as a form of sacrifice to become closer to God. We can fast from anything that distracts us and submit to Him as a form of love, oneness, and death to ourselves, just as Jesus did for us. Jesus denied a momentary comfort.

What are you comforting yourself with that the enemy wants you to be distracted and numbed by? Is it your phone, gossip, pornography, alcohol, drugs, or anger? Maybe it's something you deem as simple or ok, like a purse or shoes. As I said earlier in the book, sometimes we cannot relieve these spirits of their dwelling unless we are fasting and or, deep in prayer.

The many women who laid hands on me and relieved me of an entity at the silent retreat were just as important as my fasting. They too, were in the right mindset to lay hands on someone.

The woman with the blood disorder just touched Jesus' robe, and because her faith was so strong and His presence so immense, she was healed. Sometimes our relationship is so strong and our faith so great that he can do amazing things.

It's not only about what you are comforting yourself with but what you are watching. The spirit of fear can enter if you're letting yourself watch a lot of scary movies and if you let your children watch them. What about anything with witchcraft?

Look at it this way, I'll paint a picture for you when it comes to what you're listening to, and it can also pertain to what you're watching.

You're driving and you start listening to old clubbing songs, and it reminds you of those days when you used to drop it like it's hot and back it up to a complete stranger while holding the fifth drink you swore you wouldn't order. Now your mind is envisioning yourself dancing, and you may even start to crave a drink or think about how it would be fun to go out and drink and dance with some friends.

This next particular day, you are driving, listening to music, and you hear a country song that makes you want a bonfire, beer, and a lake. I'll even throw in a S'more for you.

The next country song makes you upset because it's sad, and you remember when the love of your life broke up with you, or you went through a divorce, and this song played at work during that difficult time and made you upset, and now you're crying and reliving all of the hurt.

Maybe another song comes on like Shania Twain's, *Man I Feel Like a Woman,* and now you want to kick a door down and fight someone. You're going to go home and just stare at your husband with eyes of fire all because Shania said, "LET'S GO, GIRLS!" The poor man doesn't even know why you're staring at him, nor does he deserve such aggressive treatment.

Maybe next is a praise and worship song that makes you take a deep breath. It's calming, and as you sing along, you're proclaiming words of love to God, and then you sense the Holy Spirit is present, sending chills down your spine. You may even start crying because you're overwhelmed with life, or maybe the presence of God is overwhelming you with happiness, but you know that even if your tears are from hurts, He weeps with you. You begin to pray or to ask Him questions, and before you know it, you've spent time with the Lord.

How can I depict from these examples? Well, duh, because I've done it.

A song came out a while back with a very catchy chorus, and the song was about shooting another child for his shoes. I refused to allow it in my home. The "oh, it's just a song" wasn't going to fly.

Look at what happens to our feelings, mind, and emotions when we worship at church or at home. What can happen mentally and emotionally when a child is walking around singing about shooting another student for his shoes?

Let's just acknowledge that one song can cause you to lift your hands while another song can cause you to lift your middle finger.

I found my oldest son curled up in a ball on his bedroom floor, listening to music that was pelting his emotions in all the wrong ways. He has a musical mind, and while God meant it for good, he has turned from God because of his hurts and chooses to live a life away from Him, but it's ok because my faith in his return to Christ is immense.

That day I found him in a ball listening to music, he was suicidal. I had to take him to the hospital and from there, he spent a week in a mental institute.

I'm not saying that a pastor has never taken his own life or that you can't listen to Shania Twain. I'm not saying I don't ever have a glass of wine, but for me, that isn't an addiction. I am saying that you need to be aware of what you are listening to, watching, and feeding your mind. This isn't a book of perfection. This is a book of awareness.

Who are you around? Iron sharpens iron (Proverbs 27:17), and I'm pretty sure most of us have a friend or someone in our lives that we can say, without a doubt, doesn't suit us or do us any good even if it felt like they did.

I've had friends that get me, we laugh and have a great time together, but we went down different paths and that led me to end certain friendships. I know when someone seems to pull me in the wrong direction.

I also know that there have been plenty of times in my life when I made huge mistakes as a friend, stranger, and even sister that have caused people to look upon me poorly. I've been someone who has sabotaged a friendship before. But, I've grown, and now, being a believer, I can forgive myself and I've been given grace from those who have forgiven me.

At the end of the day, who we chose to be around should lift us and not lower us. Proverbs 12:26 (ESV) "One who is righteous is a guide to his neighbor, but the way of the wicked leads them astray."

I'm sure Jesus made close friends with His disciples and even many of His followers. Something I've always found beautiful about Jesus was that He was able to wash the feet of the man He *KNEW* would betray Him. I think it's one of the most profound examples in the Bible, especially in today's world where we get upset over someone taking our parking spot.

Imagine someone taking your parking spot you had been waiting for, and instead of speeding off and screaming at them, you park and wait for them to go into the store. Then, you wash their car for them and leave a note about how much you love them. It's a minor example compared to turning someone in to the authorities to face their future death, but you get my point.

COMMON SPIRITS

Let me just start by saying there's a vast majority of spirits and studies that I cannot even begin to grasp. I am by no means laying this out because I feel that I'm some sort of an expert on this subject.

But through Scripture, research, personal experience, and family history, I can assure you I do know a little something. I think the little something I do know needs to be shared because you may find yourself doing some of the things listed here.

Remember, this isn't all of the unclean spirits, this is just some common suggestions and defiantly a few that I've dealt with. You may see some of your weaknesses in these, and that doesn't necessarily mean you have that spirit, it just means you're human, and the enemy does know where you are weak but getting to know yourself and knowing how God designed you will keep your weaknesses at bay. However, if you find you have a lot of these and display them often, then you may have these unclean spirits.

***JEZEBEL SPIRIT*-** This is something I dealt with and denied for a long time. Not on purpose, but because I was too veiled to see how it was hindering myself and those around me. When we control ourselves, we tend to do it as a form of self-protection. Maybe you have developed something like OCD because of your need to control even yourself.

Jezebel was a wicked queen and wife to King Ahab. She was known for murder and sexual promiscuity. She was acknowledged for leading Israel astray towards idols.

Before you freak out, please know that I don't think you're evil, and it's highly unlikely you have murdered someone. So, what are some of the unattractive signs of having a Jezebel Spirit?

- Controlling
- Domineering
- Hatred
- Sexual immorality
- Promiscuity
- Idolatry
- False teaching
- Unrepentant sin

ORPHAN SPIRIT- Have you ever been abandoned? Dealt with feeling unloved and unwanted? Ever felt like God didn't love you or need you?

I think that many people have dealt with feeling like they didn't fit in or didn't have enough friends. This goes beyond that, I'm not talking about the fact that I can be a socially awkward person around a group of people who know each other well, and I'm the oddball out. I'm speaking about being abandoned in some way or another, which may cause you to deal with some of these characteristics of an orphan spirit. You could have grown up in the foster system or had a sibling that was the golden child, and you always felt left out.

- Always competing
- A need to stand out
- Taking satisfaction in the weakness of others
- Isolation
- A feeling of not belonging
- A need for independence
- A constant need for validation
- Lack of confidence
- Rejection issues
- Workaholic
- A drive to always perform well
- Always mistrust others

SPIRIT OF PRIDE- We live in a world where we are to take pride in a lot of things. Our children, how much money we have, the house we live in, and what we do for a living. We hear things like, "Take pride in all you do." There is sinful pride and positive pride. It's ok to feel proud of a child that just received a scholarship for their hard work. But bragging about it and holding your child up on a pedestal isn't the way to go.

It's ok to feel proud about a promotion you received at work that you worked hard for but remember to give God all the glory. God gave your child those talents to get that scholarship that other children don't have.

We've all had prideful moments in our lives, but continuous pride or bragging from a spirit of pride looks like this:

- Constantly finding fault in others and never looking at yourself
- A harsh spirit that speaks of another person's sins with irritation, annoyance, or judgment
- Being superficial
- Defensiveness
- Attention seeking
- Neglecting others

SPIRIT OF ENVY- The new cars, great career, the big house, you name it, and we have all wanted something we don't have. Sometimes I envy, and I have to catch it and correct myself. Do you want to know what I catch myself envying the most? It's that perfect body at the beach or on TV, but it's different now, unlike before I would obsess over it. I might say something to myself as a young person walks by, like, "Well, there goes me before three kids." I used to have an eating disorder when I was in my late teens and early twenties. While my weight is something that has always gone up and down, I don't have a spirit of envy that leads me to destruction anymore.

Thinking that it would be awesome to have a certain car isn't wrong. I watch HGTV and drool over some of the houses, and it's ok because they are after all, beautiful. But, I'm humble and thankful for what I do have. Are you obsessed with these symptoms?

- Comparison of relationships
- Obsession with success
- Obsession with image
- Obsession with status
- Envious emotions

OTHER COMMON SPIRITS-

- SPIRIT OF WRATH- Thinking people are not good enough or thinking you're better than other people. Being angry all the time might be something you deal with as well.
- SPIRIT OF GREED- You can experience greed for food, money, and power. This can cause you to be insensitive and destructive.
- SPIRIT OF LUST- This can go hand in hand with a Jezebel Spirit with an intense sexual craving, an intense craving in general. Lust can cause possession issues. Lust can cause you to make decisions in a relationship before you actually love someone.
- SPIRIT OF UNFORGIVENESS- Is being unable to forgive others when you yourself have been forgiven. Believing that forgiveness will make another's mistake ok. Unforgiveness can lead to being malicious and vindictive. It lurks in our homes and causes destruction to ourselves and the demise of many families. *The spirit of unforgiveness is extremely underestimated, in my opinion.*

The list of spirits can go on and on, the spirit of addiction, gluttony, perversion, etc. Look at the man in Mark 5 in the Bible who held in him 2,000 unclean spirits that caused him so much torment that he cut himself for relief. Many children and teens cut themselves today as a cry for help. This man was living in what we know today as a graveyard. When we die, our demonic spirits don't stay with our bodies, they look for a new home. He was being pelted with more and more spirits because he was in a graveyard! While that's fascinating, you're probably not living in a graveyard, but you must deal with these unclean spirits.

FAMILIAR SPIRITS AND GENERATIONAL CURSES

Familiar spirits are little boogers that study you! You keep hearing me say that Satan knows your weaknesses. This is why and it's because he has an army, and they can cling to you for generations! Ever wonder why it "Runs in the family?" Maybe your family says things like, "We're just all hot heads, and it runs in the family." Or maybe you've always wondered why alcoholism runs in your family.

How about mediums and psychics? It is definitely fascinating how they know all the things. They know when and how your dad died and want you to know that your dad said hello and that he was sorry.

The information they are receiving is deceiving because they're getting it from familiar spirits that they are in contact with. The spirit knows you and what goes on in your life. There's a reason the Bible forbids you to be involved with mediums and psychics. This can let in a whole lot of things you don't want in your life.

My mother and grandmother would visit psychics often as well as my mom would stand in the checkout line at the grocery store and read her horoscope. I went with my mother and grandmother when I was nineteen years old to a psychic and found it creepy, interesting, but creepy.

When I sat down to get a reading from this woman she knew things about me that a stranger couldn't possibly know. She had two dogs that sat behind a gate and as she began to give me information about myself the dogs would look up and around the room and begin to bark.

The psychic said there was a little girl that wanted to say hello, and that she was a class mate of mine that had died when I was younger. I kid you not, when I was in fourth grade a class mate of mine died when she was struck by the school bus one foggy morning.

She proceeded to tell me other things and then ended the session by asking me if I wanted to know when I was going to die. I, being nineteen and not knowing any better said, "I guess." She told me that I would die at eighty three of natural causes.

This is not of God, He warns against this and in no way shape or form did this information that she brought to me, bring any sort of help to the kingdom of God. It was irrelevant creepy information given to her by familiar spirits.

This is not the same as the Holy Spirit speaking to you as a vessel for God's Kingdom to bring a word to someone or to have a revelation.

1 Corinthians 14:3 (ESV) says, "On the other hand, the one who prophesies speaks to people for their upbuilding and encouragement and consolation."

Prophecy builds up the church with encouragement, and you hearing that your deceased grandpa says hello may be comforting but it is not of God and it brings zero value to you as the Bride of Christ.

I also touched an Ouija board in my middle school days, and because of these two events and the fact that my mother and grandmother visited this life often could be a tiny portion of reasoning for some of my attacks and oppression in life.

I say tiny portion because some of it goes back beyond my mother and grandmother.

I know this seems like a lot, I do, but the spirit realm is no joke and it's more vast than we can comprehend. It's happening all around us at all times.

2 Corinthians 3:17 (NLT) says, "For the Lord is the Spirit, and wherever the Spirit of the Lord is, there is freedom."

This is a great example of what's around you and there is freedom when the Spirit is present. If you're a believer, then you are one with Christ. That means that Christ is living within you. If you pulled Him out of you and had a day to spend with Him in person, where would you take Him?

I personally think it would be fun to see Jesus on a go-cart or teach Him how to drive. Maybe get Him a pair of pants. Either way, my point is that you wouldn't take Him to do shots. You wouldn't drag Him around to the bar to show everyone how your new friend can turn water into wine, so that you can look good.

Would you take Him with you to watch pornography or to watch a horror film, probably not, so if He's *IN YOU*, aren't you taking Him *WITH YOU*? And everywhere you go at that? What atmosphere are you in and creating? Because it's either of God or it's demonic.

STRONGHOLDS

Strongholds are walls of resistance that you've created for protection. The definition of a stronghold is a place that has been fortified so as to protect against an attack. Or a place where a particular cause is strongly defended or challenges that have kept you bound for years that were difficult and discouraging.

Basically, the spirits listed above can cause us to live a life full of strongholds or walls that we use to protect ourselves. Are you the person who makes fun of other people feeling worried that if you don't, they will make fun of you first? You may act that way because you spent the entire third grade being humiliated and bullied, so now you have an attitude of "I'll get them, before they get me." But now you've grown up and taken that strong hold into your marriage.

Strongholds are unhealthy promises we make for ourselves that we think are protecting us, but eventually, they hinder us.

If someone is calling you names, you can either leave or create a healthy boundary, but the problem is when you create a stronghold, and you carry that stronghold into the next relationship, or we can withdraw and not confront the person hurting us. It's a hindrance because maybe that person is trying to apologize, and you can't forgive because your father did it to you, and your trauma was never resolved. The point is that they come from self and are not of God and can be broken when relying on Him as your rock.

When we have strongholds, we develop habitual patterns of thought.

2 Corinthians 10:3-5 (NLT) reads:

> "We are human, but we don't wage war as humans do. We use God's mighty weapons, not worldly weapons, to knock down the STRONGHOLDS of human reasoning and to destroy false arguments. We destroy every proud obstacle that keeps people from knowing God. We capture their rebellious thoughts and teach them to obey Christ."

Let's read the last part again, "We capture their rebellious thoughts and teach them to obey Christ." This is speaking of tearing down the strongholds against God and rebellion of the things of this world. But we can use it towards ourselves as well. So, you capture a thought, a proud obstacle, and rebellion, and we replace it with what Christ says, which would be the opposite of pride and rebellion. An example would be obedience or humble.

It doesn't matter if you said it or if it was said to you by another person; it's a thought that can become like a revolving door.

I remember going to the county fair growing up and this one ride, in particular, was so traumatizing that I almost threw up on it. It spun you around and around so fast that gravity took over, and you could no longer move your body which was being splattered into a disgusting patted wall that probably had never been cleaned, while laughing so hard that you could barely stand. Then as you exit the ride, you are pelted with the smell of all the fried fair food mixed with your jumbled-up brain that's asking you, why? Why would you do that to me?

I can only imagine that's what happens when our mind and body encounter strongholds and we spin out of control, causing confusion. Your only release is Jesus and a commitment to never get on that ride again. Capture your stronghold, confess it and replace it with God's truth.

HEALING TRAUMA

Our lives are full of trauma, some long hauls, and some moments of trauma. As I mentioned before, I don't like the feeling of attention on me 90% of the time, and I've had to learn to take a compliment with love and grace and accept it for truth. Sometimes receiving a compliment doesn't feel comfortable to me because I was an early bloomer who had all eyes on her in school and I was taller than everyone else and had curves and a menstrual cycle at ten years old.

I was the biggest girl in my dance class in sixth grade and one day, in front of the whole class, the instructor announced that they would have to order my costume in a women's size. The problem was that the rest of the girls were tiny little things that hadn't bloomed yet, and I was the girl that sprouted over the course of a couple summers and continued to sprout into eighth grade, making me look different my freshman year of high school, which caused boys to take notice and no confidence to deal with it.

As a result of attention and no confidence, my sophomore year of high school was a doozy. I ended up pregnant and had to walk the halls of my high school, feeling alone and isolated. I was dealing with a situation that you should share with a husband, but instead, I was a child pregnant with a child in school, and all the boys I had crushes on were pointing at me, creating unwanted attention. My life has been full of unwanted interactions; some of them were created by me, while some weren't.

It was traumatic raising a baby at sixteen along with watching your parents argue every day and never show affection for each other. It was traumatic being sexually abused and having to go to a hospital at twelve years old and having a rape kit performed on you by complete strangers.

Whether at home, school, work, or in a relationship, we have probably experienced trauma at some point in our lives.

These moments that we give a lifetime to can cause insecurities and those rob you of your full potential as a believer, wife, friend, mother, and co-worker.

When you ask someone, "Why does that make you uncomfortable?" And they respond with, "I don't know," with a refusal to tell you why. It's because they think that the source of their insecurity is too little, stupid, simple, and unworthy of such insecurity. Find the source of your insecurity and deal with it no matter how small or insignificant you think it is.

SET FREE

Satan has an army. He knows your weaknesses, yes, that is true, but he's also nothing but a fly on the wall. Sometimes a horsefly and sometimes a gnat but either way, if you are a believer who wants him gone, you have the authority to tell him to leave. Get behind me, move out of my way, get out of my home and leave me alone, I'm trying to sleep!

Are the spirits I spoke of something to ignore and just whatever because we have authority? No, it's actually very serious, but I want you to understand our power because Satan knows your power, and he doesn't like it one bit.

Mark 16:17 (NLT) says, "These miraculous signs will accompany those who believe: They will cast out demons in my name, and they will speak in new languages."

Luke 10:19-20 (NLT) reads:

> "Look, I have given you authority over all the power of the enemy, and you can walk among snakes and scorpions and crush them. Nothing will injure you. But, don't rejoice because evil spirits obey you; rejoice because your names are registered in Heaven."

Please remember that we are but a human borrowing this body for a temporary time on earth. It is Jesus that lives within us, and through Jesus' authority, we use the power to cast down and cast away evil spirits. Remember, *EVERYTHING* comes back to God's glory. It is only through Him that we do everything and anything.

When you cast something away, you need to mean it. You suit up in your armor as a representative of Jesus Himself.

HELMET OF SALVATION- Is going with the Lord to work out every part of our salvation; the battle of our mind is what the enemy is coming for. It must be protected. (Ephesians 6:17)

1. Surrender thoughts that don't line up with Scripture. Casting down lies! (Colossians 3:2).
2. Wash your mind with the renewing of God's Word daily (Romans 12:2).

THE BELT OF TRUTH- (Ephesians 6:14) everything comes down to the truth. That's why I named this chapter emet for truth, because everything is attached to truth. If the devil is the father of lies, then it's important for our lives and our salvation to know the truth, which is the opposite of a lie.

1. Pray with God's Word so that truth is on your lips.
2. Start to memorize Scripture so that you can access truth immediately.

THE BREASTPLATE OF RIGHTEOUSNESS- (Ephesians 6:14) righteousness means to be made right, and we need the righteousness of Christ to carry us through life and to access and use our gifts. Righteousness allows for obedience.

1. Obey instructions from the Lord.
2. Have your community pray for you if you feel like obedience is something you struggle with and know that obedience isn't

always easy. Remember, Jonah didn't want to do what he was asked as well as many others in the Bible.

THE GOSPEL OF PEACE (SHOES)–(Ephesians 6:15) peace is God, and peace comes from God. Peace is a gift that can surpass all understanding. I can worry like there is no tomorrow if I allow it to take hold. That is defiantly not peace, the enemy wants to rob us of peace with our worry and anxiety.

Set your identity in Him by knowing who you are, to do that, make sure you walk yourself through the tools that I gave you. Taking all of the tests and writing down the results.

1. Remove anything in life that causes you to not have peace. We still need jobs, and we still need our spouses, so don't go throwing those away, but if meal prepping brings you peace, prep it. If praying over your home and children will bring you peace, then do it.
2. Create a home of peace by playing praise and worship and talking about God daily.

THE SHEILD OF FAITH- (Ephesians 6:16) we must build faith by hearing the Word of God. (Romans 10:17) We are supposed to always have it on our lips, on our minds, and on our hearts. Our faith will be tested to build endurance, and because of that, we must spend time with God.

1. Ask God for more opportunities to display your faith and build it.
2. Do exercises that will build faith, like a daily devotional, praying with a friend daily, or getting in a sermon each day.

THE SWORD OF THE SPIRIT- (Ephesians 6:17) the sword of the spirit is the Word of God. You use the Word of God to defeat the enemy. Jesus used Scripture to defeat the enemy when He was tempted in the wilderness.

Use the Word of God to defeat the enemy!

Let's look at some Scripture for a list of encouragement when it comes to our authority. Remember, authority is a DEMAND and not a question.

"Then Jesus came close to them and said, "All the authority in Heaven and on earth has been given to me." Matthew 28:18-20 (ESV)

1. "And you will know the truth, and the truth will set you free." John 8:32 (NLT)
2. "The weapons we fight with are not the weapons of the world. On the contrary, they have the divine power to demolish strongholds." 2 Corinthians 10:4 (NIV)
3. "I can do all things through Christ who strengthens me." Philippians 4:13 (NKJV)
4. "Have you forgotten that your body is now the sacred temple of the Spirit of Holiness, who lives in you? You don't belong to yourself any longer, for the gift of God, the Holy Spirit, lives inside your sanctuary." 1 Corinthians 6:19 (TPT)

RECAP: A LIST OF THINGS WE CAN DO TO CAST OUT EVIL SPIRITS, BREAK STRONGHOLDS AND HEAL FROM TRAUMA!!!

1. Believe in your heart that Jesus is Lord and confess it with your mouth daily.
2. Seek out therapy

3. Go to trusted people at church; if they fail, don't let it hinder you, find a church!
4. Be in the Word of God daily.
5. Speak against the enemy.
6. Gather like-minded people who will fast with you and lay hands on you
7. Once you are healed and turn away from something, don't turn back to it.
8. Stay around like-minded people for fellowship, prayer, and support.
9. Cast entities away from yourself.
10. Create a home that has God in it
    1. Praying
    2. Singing
    3. Studying
    4. Praise and worship music

11.) Ask God for the baptism of the Holy Spirit so you can use a special language between you and your creator.

At the end of the day, everything is up to us. The enemy isn't afraid of us if we do not use the Word of God. We see this in Acts 19:13-16 (NLT)

> "A group of Jews was traveling from town to town casting out evil spirits. They tried to use the name of the Lord Jesus in their incantation, saying, "I command you in the name of Jesus whom Paul preaches to come out." Seven sons of Sceva, a leading priest, were doing this. But one time, when they tried it, the evil spirit said, "I know Jesus, and I know Paul, but who are you?"

Just being a priest isn't good enough. The Bible just sitting somewhere isn't good enough. Remember when I said that I slept next to my Bible the night I was attacked at the retreat? Did it work? No, I was attacked for the second time. So, go dust off your Bible or download it to your phone and dive into it!

Prayer

Heavenly Father,
I come to you and praise you for all of the protection you've placed upon me. I ask that you awaken my mind and heart to any unclean spirits that may be keeping me from a full and plentiful relationship with you and those around me. Reveal to me any strongholds that are keeping me down and compressed. Thank you, Jesus, for your steps that lead me to progress in becoming free from all hurt, harm, and danger.
In Jesus' name, Amen

CHAPTER 8
Who Is Jesus?

*I*f I am who I am, and I am who Jesus says I am, then who is Jesus? Say what now? Listen, my point is that we're Christians, and literally followers of Christ. I think it's important to look over the life of Jesus and dive into the man that we follow and strive to be like, Jesus came as a reflection in the flesh!

John 1:14 (NLT) reads;

> "So the Word became human and made His home among us. He was full of unfailing love and faithfulness. And we have seen His glory, the glory of the Father's one and only son."

He came to serve, Matthew 20:28 (NLT). "For even the Son of Man came not to be served but to serve others and to give his life as a ransom for many"

Matthew 16:13-16 (NLT) says:

> "When Jesus came to the region of Caesarea Philippi, He asked His disciples, "Who do people say that the Son of Man is?" "Well," They replied, "Some say John the Baptist, some say Elijah, and others say Jeremiah or one of the other prophets." "Then

He asked them, "But who do you say I am?" Simon Peter answered, "You are the Messiah, the Son of the living God."

Mark 6:1-5 (TPT) says:

"Afterward, Jesus left Capernaum and returned with his disciples to Nazareth, his hometown. On the Sabbath, he went to teach in the synagogue. Everyone who heard his teaching was overwhelmed with astonishment. They said among themselves, "What incredible wisdom has been given to him! Where did he receive such profound insights? And what mighty miracles flow through his hands! Isn't this Mary's son, the carpenter, the brother of Jacob, Joseph, Judah, and Simon? And don't his sisters all live here in Nazareth?" And they took offense at him.

"Jesus said to them, "A prophet is treated with honor everywhere except in his own hometown, among his relatives, and in his own house." He was unable to do any great miracle in Nazareth except to heal a few sick people by laying His hands upon them. He was amazed at the depth of their unbelief."

I guess you could say, "Rumor has it" Jesus was just a carpenter's son. He was just a dude from Nazareth, and it didn't matter how anointed His message was or who He healed. He was up against His hometown.

Rumor has it that I'm just a confused, promiscuous girl who had a baby as a teenager in a small town in Michigan.

Who people say you are, and what people think you are, is not who God says you are, and your past decisions do not define you! Who I was in high school and even six months ago are not the same person. It's funny how people can hold on to who they think you are without ever knowing you! They just know *OF* you, or they have *HEARD* about you.

Yes, Jesus worked and had a job as a handyman before He started His ministry at thirty years old. How ridiculous that His own hometown couldn't see past that and looked down on Him, which blocked their blessings from Him! So, chat it up, Kathy, because you could be blocking your blessings!

Jesus was brought into this world step by step the way we were. Ok, ok, your mom probably wasn't a virgin when she got pregnant with you, but aside from that, He was a baby who needed His mother, and He had an adoptive father and siblings who probably picked on Him. He had friends and learned to read and write. Jesus had a job to serve others and contribute to His home.

He was tempted by the enemy just like us, and He was asked to walk out His calling just like us.

Jesus was also a passionate man.

Mark 10:14 (TPT) reads:

> "When Jesus saw what was happening, he became indignant with his disciples and said to them, "Let all the little children come to me and never hinder them! Don't you know that God's kingdom exists for such as these?"

It says He was "indignant," which is to become angry, hot, or feel the wrath of something unfair or unjust. But, please notice He didn't resort to punching anyone or violence of any sort in this particular moment even though I'm sure He wanted to. I would gather that Jesus probably saw some punch-able faces in His day; I'm just saying.

However, in another instance, Jesus went into the temple courtyard and noticed some unwanted goods and services going on.

John 2:15-16 (TPT) says:

> "So, Jesus found some cords and made them into a whip. Then he drove out every one of them and their animals from the courtyard of the temple, and he kicked over their tables filled with money, scattering it everywhere! "And he told the merchants 'Get these things out of here!' Don't you dare commercialize my Father's house."

Now before you start to think you can't order a coffee at church or buy a book from your book store at church, Jesus was angry about the heart of the people in the courtyard. Not only were they blocking a passageway to the temple for those who were there for the right reasons, but they were greedy as well.

So, He whipped their butts into shape! Also, a huge side note, whipping people today is frowned upon. Don't let me catch a news article about someone whipping people because they were passionate and one with Christ. Ok?

So does that mean that Jesus was a hypocrite when it comes to Ephesians 4:26 (NLT) "And "don't sin by letting anger control you"?

The problem is that we stop right there. The whole Scripture reads, "And "Don't sin by letting anger control you. "Don't let the sun go down while you are still angry."

Jesus didn't have an anger problem, it doesn't say that He continued to be angry and gave everyone the silent treatment for three days afterward, refusing to teach. It doesn't say that He was angry often. He did get frazzled, annoyed, frustrated, and passionate. Look what He was up against. Jesus was not controlled by His anger even when He had strong emotions or times of anger, He didn't always act on them.

Not letting the sun go down doesn't just apply to a spouse. It applies to any relationship in your life, including your kids. Ephesians 4:27 (TPT) says, "Don't give the slanderous accuser, the Devil, an opportunity to manipulate you!"

Letting that sun go down allows for the enemy to take root with his manipulation and lies. Think of the enemy as a hook to catch you and Jesus as an anchor that keeps you stable.

I'm aware that anger can nestle itself deep within; I mean, women do tend to say "nothing" when asked what's wrong. Are we exhausted from asking in the first place? Do we want attention?

Maybe we have needs that we assume won't be met, so we just say, nothing. Life can be exhausting, there is no doubt about it. Coming to a mutual agreement and knowing it will at least be resolved soon or working towards an outcome is what a lot of the process should look like, and that's ok. It's letting that anger manifest and take over the mind, which in return changes hearts, and that becomes the problem.

Jesus was so passionate because He is the way, and anyone who got in the way was a distraction from the enemy. John 14:6 (TPT) reads,

> "I am the Way, I am the Truth, and I am the Life. No
> one comes next to the Father except through union
> with me. To know me is to know my Father too."

We must have eyes that see and ears that hear (Matthew 13:16). There's a reason that Jesus told His disciples to move along if people were not willing to listen (Matthew 10:14) and it's because you have to believe in your heart (John 3:16). Jesus knew His time was limited, and He had a job to do. There were too many people to reach who were eager to listen.

It's a pretty important job to be the Way. I'm passionate that Jesus died for me, but I cannot even begin to imagine knowing I was about to go through a crucifixion to be the Way.

Even through His passion and table tipping moment, He had compassion. John 4:6 (TPT) reads, "Wearied by his long journey, he sat on the edge of Jacob's well, and sent his disciples into the village to buy food, for it was already afternoon."

Jesus was "wearied," which means He was exhausted in strength. He was probably extremely thirsty and hungry because He sent His disciples to get food. He asked the Samaritan woman to give Him a drink. The Scripture says He sat on the edge of the well. He didn't stand; He had to sit because He was tired.

Jesus didn't have to speak to anyone, especially a Samaritan woman. All the man wanted was some water and a snacky-snack. He could have just said, "Woman, get me water now!" And meant actual water even though it wasn't custom for Jews to speak to Samaritans. I believe it probably had a double meaning because I'm sure Jesus did drink some water.

My sister and I have this thing about us needing water and needing it now! When I need water, it's as if my whole world stops, and I need to get to it now. I won't lie, I've been known to be a completely different person when I'm hungry. Unfortunately, I also get to put thirsty into that category.

The amount of compassion He had to have had when it came to her life and to lay down His *ACTUAL* thirst even for a second had to have been intense. What a beautiful moment of love and compassion to lay down His desires and minister to a woman that was a used waste according to her society. Sometimes, as believers, we don't get the privilege of being *SELFISH* because we are responsible for our *SELFLESS* moments leading others to Christ. But this is who Jesus was; it was His job, His purpose.

John 11:33-35 (TPT) reads:

> "When Jesus looked at Mary and saw her weeping at his feet, and all her friends who were with her grieving, he shuddered with emotion and was deeply moved with tenderness and compassion. He said to them, "Where did you bury him?" "Lord, come with us, and we'll show you." They replied. "Then, Tears streamed down Jesus' face.

He raised Lazarus from the dead. He wept with His friends, He didn't use His power to put Himself in a high and mighty position. He could have easily not been bothered by the children coming to Him. He took in every moment as an opportunity to minister and showcase His love.

Matthew 8:2-3 (TPT) reads:

> "Suddenly, a leper walked up to Jesus and threw himself down before him in worship and said, "Lord, you have the power to heal me, if you really want to." "Jesus reached out His hand and touched the leper and said, "Of course, I want to heal you-be healed!" And instantly, all signs of leprosy disappeared!"

Leprosy was a skin condition that would disfigure people physically and condemn them morally. They were deemed unclean and had a process to go through to be accepted back into society.

It's 2022, and you can't tell me you haven't side-eyed another human being in the past two years for just coughing. Jesus says, "Of course, I'll heal you. No problem, I've got you!"

Jesus spent time with people the world would reject. No one liked tax collectors back then. Not only did they take your taxes which are law, and we have to pay them. But they would take beyond what was owed and have no remorse or compassion while doing so. We can see in Luke 19:1-10 that a man named Zacchaeus was extremely interested in Jesus. He was a tax collector, and being tall probably wasn't on his dating app. He couldn't see over people, so he climbed a fig tree to get a better look at Jesus.

Jesus called him out by name and basically said, "Let's do dinner at your place." Everyone was annoyed, and I could just picture Zacchaeus skipping by with a smile on his face and not a care in the world because Jesus was coming to dinner.

He asked for forgiveness and offered to pay anyone he had done wrong back times four. Jesus took heart to his change of heart, and Zacchaeus' life was changed forever. Zacchaeus may have been short but it takes a big person to admit you're wrong, turn from it and then better yourself.

Nothing can separate us from His love. Romans 8:35 (TPT) says:

"Who could ever divorce us from the endless love of God's Anointed One? Absolutely no one! For nothing in the universe has the power to diminish His love toward us. Troubles, pressures, and problems are unable to come between us and Heaven's love. What about persecutions, deprivations, dangers, and death threats? No, for they are all impotent to hinder omnipotent love."

His love for us is forever and always, and there's nothing we can do that will stop Him from loving us. Every now and then, it feels as though we have done things that would make Him lose sight of His love for us. We may even feel unworthy of it. But it's just not true.

Community is important, they say it takes a village to raise a child. I say it takes a village to stay dedicated to your faith. Even if you're like me, an introverted extrovert, the community is important to keeping our walk, worked out.

Hebrews 10:24-25 (TPT) reads:

> "Discover creative ways to encourage others and to motivate them toward acts of compassion, doing beautiful works as expressions of love. This is not the time to pull away and neglect meeting together, as some have formed the habit of doing. In fact, we should come together even more frequently, eager to encourage and urge each other onward as we anticipate that day dawning."

Jesus created the church, and He had people around Him all of the time. He didn't set out on this mission by Himself, ignoring everyone and keeping to Himself. He had friends, disciples, and followers, He preached to crowds and read the Word of God. He taught us how to be towards one another.

Your community and your tribe are important. We have seasons where we may lose people who hurt us or even have seasons where we can't get to those women's groups. I understand that for some, plugging in is hard to do, but I recommend doing it.

If you're like me and are tempted by the enemy to even have a bad day, then you need people in your life who can snap you out of it. You need people who will pray for you and lift you up.

Romans 12:4-5 (TPT) says:

> "In the human body there are many parts and organs, each with a unique function. And so it is in the body of Christ. For though we are many, we've all been mingled into one body in Christ. This means that we are all vitally joined to one another, with each contributing to the others."

The gifts that God has given you are not only to be shared and used to bring people to Christ but to be used to keep us in Christ.

And best of all is Matthew 18:20 (TPT) says, "For wherever two or three come together in honor of my name, I am right there with them."

There is power in more than one!

Listen, I talk to people all day long at work and have children. I completely understand that it gets to crowded out there and it's scary.

Unless you're my ex-husband (I'm sorry, he's just a funny example, don't worry, he knows I put these things in here) but the man likes to talk. Women say, "Get you a man who talks." I say, "Proceed with caution". I joke around that my ex would talk to a tree if he thought it was listening, or even if he didn't. It came in handy when I did want to talk, but also, he's a people person and people are drawn to him in that way, and it's how God made him. So, I understand that not everyone is made the same when it comes to community.

I think some of it as well can be because of insecurities. People don't want to be judged for what they've done. They are afraid to get close to people. But I promise you, if Jesus always had people around. You should consider a community.

When I invite people to church and they respond with, "Oh, I can't go, I'd catch fire." I always reply with, "I promise, if I haven't caught fire, you're probably safe."

You can't tell by looking at me what I've been through, you can only judge me by thinking I will judge you, based on what *YOU'VE* been through. Basically, what I am saying is that your fear of judgment will cause you to judge others. Do we have plenty of judgmental Christians in the church? Absolutely, but don't let them win!

People don't like to go to church for fear they will be judged. They fear that the church is full of perfect people who have never done a thing wrong, and feel they won't belong.

John 3:20 (NLT) says: "All who do evil hate the light and refuse to go near it for FEAR THEIR SINS WILL BE EXPOSED."

Don't believe me? Don't think this old book, the Bible, pertains to us today? Pick up your phone and Google the top five to ten reasons why people don't go to church. You'll find multiple sites to choose from that will inform you, in no particular order, that:

1. They practice their believes in other ways
2. They don't feel welcomed
3. *FEAR THEY WILL BE JUDGED*
4. Church is boring
5. They don't believe
6. Too much hypocrisy (which Jesus warns against)

So, Jesus is love, compassion, passion, a teacher, leader, and truth-teller, and He is the Way! He modeled who and how we should be every step of the way.

And last but not least, Mark 11:12-14 (TPT) reads:

> "The Next day as he left Bethany, Jesus was feeling
> HUNGRY. He noticed a leafy fig tree in the

distance, so he walked over to see if there was any fruit on it, but there was none, only leaves (for it wasn't yet the season for bearing figs). Jesus spoke to the fig tree, saying, 'NO ONE WILL EVER EAT FRUIT FROM YOU AGAIN!' And the disciples overheard him."

This Scripture right here is the first-ever recording of someone being hangry. That's right, you heard me. Jesus needed a snickers, He was hangry and cursed a fig tree. It's biblically acceptable to be hangry. And with a shrug of the shoulders, I said what I said.

PERFECTIONISM IS DUMB

After reading about Jesus and how He models what our lives should look like, you might feel a little discouraged in a way. The problem is that we think we need to be at a certain place in life to start, we feel we need to have things just right, and I feel like we have all dealt with needing something to be perfect.

Maybe it's the way the kids look before leaving the house, the way your home looks, your job, and even yourself. Maybe when you cook, it has to be just right, and possibly you don't struggle with this at all.

Perfect is having all the required or desirable elements, qualities, or characteristics, or it means as good as it is possible to be. Well, that right there is why perfect, according to the world, is dumb. If perfect is as good as it is possible to be, then that means that "perfect" is in the eye of the beholder.

What is perfect to you and what is perfect to your spouse may not be the same thing. Now, you can have a standard, which is a level of quality to obtain. But you can also set your standard too high.

You tell your kids, "Pick up this room, and it better be perfect."

Well, it's probably not going to be because he's a kid, and he doesn't care if it's clean or not. However, he probably knows the standard you hold him to. Perfect to you would be how you do it, versus a standard of acceptance for him.

Continuously placing worldly perfection on yourself or those around you can lead to disappointment. Notice I had said worldly perfection.

Matthew 5:48 (TPT) says, "Since you are children of a perfect Father in Heaven, become perfect like him."

Philippians 4:8-9 (TPT) says:

> "Keep your thoughts continually fixed on all that is authentic and real, honorable and admirable, beautiful and respectful, pure and holy, merciful and kind. And fasten your thoughts on every glorious work of God, praising him always. *Put into practice* the example of all that you have heard from me or seen in my life and the God of peace will be with you in all things."

We are challenged enough in life as it is, so don't go placing worldly perfection on yourself or those you love with the house, clothes, cars, job, etc. Set standards and do everything for His glory. As you abide in Him, and *put into practice* you'll start to see with Jesus vision.

Sometimes parenting and being a spouse can feel like you're doing everything wrong. Set your earthly perfections aside and focus on His good and pleasing will for yourself, your family, your friends, and your work environment.

Our job is to be loved, love others and walk in His will. It's not to be the gatekeeper of perfection. Focus on God and focus on how Jesus taught you to be in each situation.

Prayer

Jesus,
Thank you for modeling everything for us. Our lives are meaningless with out you. Your sacrifice was the ultimate form of love. Help our minds to focus on your sacrifice and how significant it is. Continue to guide me, teach me and produce a heart in me that yearns for you.
In Jesus name, Amen.

CHAPTER 9
Doubt

*D*oubt is a feeling of uncertainty or a lack of confidence. You can immediately see how a lack of confidence works against your relationship with Jesus in 1 John 5:14 (TPT) "Since we have this CONFIDENCE, we can also have great boldness before him, for if we ask anything agreeable to his will, he will hear us." Doubt will hinder your relationship with God. It will rob your confidence in Him and in yourself.

We see it first in Genesis 3:1-7 when Eve was tricked by the enemy. She wasn't even thinking about eating the fruit that was forbidden until it was presented to her in another light. She didn't need to be interested in eating it because she had all the fruit she needed, just like she told the serpent.

I have to admit, I've doubted myself many times. Some have been restored, and some doubts I still have questions about, these are doubts that I prayed about that didn't come to light. But I wouldn't call them doubts anymore because they're a question in waiting. I'm still waiting to understand some things God has yet to reveal to me, but I have faith the answer will come, which removes the doubt.

The problem is that if I doubt, it sends me into over thinking, leading to a bunch of thoughts that I don't need to have.

James 1:5-8 (TPT) reads:

> "And if anyone longs to be wise, ask God for wisdom
> and he will give it! He won't see your lack of wisdom

as an opportunity to scold you over your failures but he will overwhelm your failures with his generous grace. Just make sure you ask empowered by CONFIDENT faith WITHOUT DOUBTING that you will receive. For the ambivalent person believes one minute and doubts the next. Being undecided makes you become like the rough seas driven and tossed by the wind. You're up one minute and tossed down the next. When you are half-hearted and wavering, it leaves you unstable. Can you really expect to receive anything from the Lord when you're in that condition?"

OUCH! That Scripture stings a bit. I'm not a human with a giant vocabulary, and I have to admit that when people use big words or uncommon words, I have to ask, "What does that mean?" So, naturally, I read this, and I'm like, "Ok Google, what's ambivalent?" How I survived before the internet, I'll never know.

An ambivalent person or a person with mixed feelings is a person who's tossed around by the wind. Jesus gave me the image of tumbleweed while thinking about doubt. When you doubt, you're like tumbleweed roaming the desert. Tumbleweed isn't just one plant rolling around, but a number of different plants (thoughts) rolled up together. It's a seed (doubts) that once mature and dry (negative thoughts that once manifested, turn into doubts), detaches from its root (God) and rolls due to the force of the wind.

I was quite astonished when I looked up tumbleweed after getting that image. How many times have you been tumbleweed detaching yourself from God? How many times a day have you been tumbleweed just flying by the seat of your pants, wandering? For me, I've doubted that others would change or that God could change them. That, in turn, can cause you to give up on people, including yourself. Doubt can be why relationships fail, doubt can be why you don't see God moving in the way you feel He should.

I know for me, when I doubt, it can allow thoughts like, "*Am I good enough?*" If we begin to doubt our quality in anything, it makes us start to think and second guess, just like Eve did in the Garden.

John 20:25-29 (TPT) says:

> "So the disciples informed him, "We have seen the Lord with our own eyes!" Still unconvinced, Thomas replied, "There's no way I'm going to believe this unless I personally see the wounds of the nails in his hands, touch them with my finger, and put my hand into the wound of his side where he was pierced!"
>
> "Then, eight days later, Thomas and all the others were in the house together. And even though all the doors were locked, Jesus suddenly stood before them! "Peace to you." He said. Then looking into Thomas' eyes, he said, "Put your finger here in the wounds of my hands. Here-put your hand into my wounded side and see for yourself. Thomas, don't give in to your doubts any longer; just believe!"

First of all, how do you come through walls or just appear and then have a solid body for someone to touch your wounds? Secondly, how do you just appear in the room and be like, "Shalom!" What's up, guys? No big deal, just stopping by so doubting Thomas here can touch my wounds. This was pure grace and love! Jesus didn't have to do this, His disciples literally got to hang out with Him in the flesh, and still, they doubted.

Maybe they were arguing over who was going to be the next greatest thing (Luke 22:24) because they knew Jesus on a personal level. Maybe they doubted because they knew Him in the flesh.

Have you ever been asked by God to do something that you didn't think was possible? Even something small can seem out of reach at times. For me, getting this far in a book, knowing who I am, and overcoming turmoil are doubts God has crushed!

But there have been times when I had doubts because I didn't understand God's timing.

Genesis 18:11-15 (NLT) says,

> "Abraham and Sarah were both very old by this time, and Sarah was long past the age of having children. So she laughed silently to herself and said, "How could a worn-out woman like me enjoy such pleasure, especially when my master, my husband, is also so old?" Then the Lord said to Abraham, "Why did Sarah laugh? Why did she say, "Can an old woman like me have a baby?" Is anything too hard for the Lord? I will return about this time next year, and Sarah will have a son." "Sarah was afraid, so she denied it, saying, "I didn't laugh." But the Lord said, "No, you did laugh."

I'm sorry, but I find the last part hilarious. It reminds me of many life scenarios, especially for me as the girl who laughs at the wrong times. I'm the friend you do NOT make eye contact with if something is funny, but you're supposed to be serious. You lock eyes with me, and it's over, I'm laughing.

Sarah chuckled, she had been praying for a child, and even though it wasn't in God's will for her to give her husband to another woman, she did so out of desperation to have a baby. Even Abraham laughed! (Genesis 17:17)

So, now that she's old and beyond childbearing years, her doubt has set in, and she laughed at the thought of God doing something that she prayed for and she thought that ship had sailed.

I have to wonder if God delayed her blessing because she took matters into her own hands with Abraham and Hagar. Or, I guess you could say she delayed her own blessing. Psalms 138:6 (NLT) says, "Though the Lord is great, he cares for the humble, but he keeps his distance from the proud."

How beautiful that even though God was like, I know these two are not laughing at me right now, He meets them at their laughter with a son named Isaac, meaning, "One who laughs."

Taking life into my own hands has never worked for me. My mood, mind, heart, and peace have always been at their very best at times in my life when I was closest to God. Revelation 3:15-16 (TPT) reads:

> "I know all that you do, and I know that you are
> neither frozen in apathy nor fervent with passion.
> How I wish you were either one or the other! But
> because you are neither cold nor hot but lukewarm,
> I am about to spit you from my mouth."

God can and will back off when you do. Going through the motions will only get you so far with His grace. But, He will always love you and welcome you back.

John 1:1 (NLT) says, "In the beginning the Word already existed, the Word was with God, and the Word was God."

There's a reason that being in God's Word creates relationships and fights doubt. It's because the Word is literally who He is, and there is no way around it. I should know I've tried every possible way around it.

Genesis 19:26 (NLT) says, "But Lot's wife looked back as she was following behind him, and she turned into a pillar of salt."

I've always found this to be a little harsh. I mean, wouldn't you want to look back? A lot (no pun intended) was going on, and everyone you knew, your home and your life, was being destroyed right behind you.

Do you have any idea how loud the destruction of an entire city must have been? I mean, Abraham was out sipping his morning cup of coffee from afar, just watching the show like it's the fourth of July! (Genesis 19:27-28 NLT)

Lot had angels sitting with him eating dinner, and then all of a sudden, the angels told him to run, and the Bible says Lot hesitated. The angels took his hand and the hands of his wife and two daughters and rushed them to safety outside the city, because the Lord was gracious to them. (Genesis 19:16 NLT)

We hear all the time, "Where was God when I needed Him?" *HE WAS HOLDING YOUR HAND, PULLING YOU!* But you want to doubt what He's telling you, because you're too afraid of where He's moving you, so you hesitate.

You keep looking back on your past, and you keep looking back on what you think you've destroyed or what someone else destroyed, and you feel that it's not reparable, and God wants you to come with Him so He can repair and make things new.

It seems so simple, almost too simple. Just run and don't look back. This has to be where they get ideas for scary movies. People always look back in scary movies. Then what happens next? They trip and fall. It's no secret I wouldn't last long in a scary movie, and I would dare to say, I may even be the first one to go based on how much I drop my keys trying to unlock a door, but would you be lots wife? Do you look back? I believe Lot's wife looked back because she couldn't believe what was happening. She looked back like, "God, are you sure?"

Do you have doubt that makes you look back on everything that was said, done, and may or may not happen? Doubt is a delay. It's a delay in healing, a delay in a relationship with God, and even a delay in our calling. Doubt kept me from so much in life. It kept me from following through with writing for twenty years!

I know someone who's funny, kind, encouraging, smart, and beautiful, and all she sees is that she's not worthy, not worthy of God's love, not worthy of progress. She thinks she's not smart enough, which has hindered her life tremendously. She doubts that God will redeem her again because she felt she gave Him her all, and her world still came crashing down. She felt alone, so she started to isolate herself, her feelings, and her heart. She doubts that God's Word actually means what it says. But she has hopes of returning to the girl she once was someday.

It's ok to question certain things, and its okay to proceed with caution in certain situations, but doubt and hope don't go together, so if you doubt but hope for something, then you lack faith.

Hebrews 11:1 (NLT) "Faith shows the reality of what we hope for; it is the evidence of things we cannot see."

Hope is a confident expectation, and doubt is a feeling of uncertainty. They are literally the opposite. Hope is not a wish. It's a matter of fact.

HOPE= CERTAINTY

DOUBT= UNCERTAINTY

As a matter of fact, I hope I do get a raise. As a matter of fact, I hope I do become a New York Times best-selling author. As a matter of fact, I hope I do purchase a home within the next two years, and so on and so on. I HOPE!

Hope in Hebrew is *Tikvah,* and it's a cord or rope meaning to bind. So, we bind together our unshakable faith using hope.

As I said, when we doubt, we delay; Proverbs 13:12 (NLT) reads,

> "Hope deferred makes the heart sick, but a dream fulfilled is a tree of life."

Our hearts can become sick from doubt that DELAYS our hope. As we begin to start searching for who we are, even if we knew at one time and have lost it or even if we have been full of doubt, God will begin to renew our hearts. Ezekiel 36:26 (NLT) says,

> "And I will give you a new heart, and I will put a new spirit in you. I will take out your stony, stubborn heart and give you a tender, responsive heart."

When we accept Christ as our Lord and Savior, remove oppression and unclean spirits and begin to study God's Word, and make leaps of faith, He will leap with us.

We have to create healthy patterns again and not with hearts of doubt but with a thankful heart;

Romans 12:2 (NLT) says:

> "Don't copy the behavior and customs of this world, but let God transform you into a new person by changing the way you think. Then you will learn to know God's will for you, which is good and pleasing and perfect."

He'll transform you! But you must be willing to listen and hear the truth.

Listening is when you give someone's voice attention, and hearing is the special sense by which noises and tones are received. So, in other words, I'm hearing your voice and giving it attention by listening.

God gives me an image when I read that, and it's of a soldier standing at attention which represents listening, and sound waves entering his ear, which represents hearing. If I'm not at attention, then I'm only hearing.

Now, if you're a mom, you have skills when it comes to this. You can hear them yelling, "MOM", but you're not listening because you have a million things to do or you told them just a minute. Ever heard someone talking but then came too and only caught the last thing they said because you trailed off into your own thoughts? Maybe you were innocent in the situation, and they had spinach in their teeth, and it's all you could focus on, but the point is hearing them talk but not listening to the words.

Did you know that hearing is the last of our senses to go when we start to pass? That's why they tell you to speak to your loved ones in an unresponsive state. God is so beautiful that He will leave hearing until the last breath so that they can still be ministered to. They can still hear a prayer, a comforting voice of a loved one, and God's Word.

A baby growing up in the womb can recognize its mother and father's voice before it enters the world because of hearing and learning the voice of loved ones. So, in essence, you hear loved ones before your first breath, and you hear loved ones before your last breath. God wants you to hear His voice and learn His voice.

I'm not talking about an audible voice from God Himself, but He speaks to us in many different ways. Even if it's through a dream, are you listening to what He's trying to tell you? Are you hearing that still small voice inside you telling you not to do something? Are you listening to that friend that God is using to confirm something you've been praying for?

Being able to hear is important. It builds our faith; Romans 10:17 (NLT) says, "So, faith comes from hearing that is, hearing the Good News about Christ."

If you're not listening or hearing, then you can't begin to let what others are telling you to penetrate your mind and, in turn, your heart. I've been that person on both ends, and not listening will hinder you. If you don't listen, confess and allow yourself to heal, then you can't hear anyone, including God. All you will hear is your trauma, and all you will respond with is your trauma.

I've been the girl who just vents and vents and doesn't allow anything coming from the other person to sink in because I'm so caught up in the emotions of the event that I circle over the hurt continuously. I had a therapist tell me one time that arguing when no one is willing to listen is like flying a plane with nowhere to land. It just keeps circling.

That's why it's best in an argument when there is only one listener, or both parties are unwilling to listen that you separate and come back when it's a healthier environment to talk.

I've also been the person listening to someone vent who won't allow your advice to absorb. Granted, we all need time to just vent but isn't healing more important even though the truth is hard?

Matthew 13:15 (NLT) reads:

> "For the hearts of these people are hardened, and their ears cannot hear, and they have closed their eyes so their eyes cannot see and their ears cannot hear, and their hearts cannot understand, and they cannot turn to me and let me heal them."

Self-reflection is an internal inspection of the heart and mind. Our actions flow from the heart and mind, and we are to seek the truth. Self-reflection causes a gross word to take place. It's a really hard word, and that word is vulnerable. Why would I call this word gross? Because it's a hard thing to do, we feel left out in the open when we have to be vulnerable. Being vulnerable to me used to feel like swimming in the ocean with sharks circling you, so naturally, people tend to retreat to safety. That doesn't mean being vulnerable is easy for me, but it's easier than it used to be.

James 5:16 (ESV) says;

> "Therefore, confess your sins to one another and pray for one another, that you may be healed. The prayer of a righteous person has great power as it is working."

Confessing your sins to someone and then asking for prayer is an extremely vulnerable thing to do, and we have to do it knowing it won't feel good at the moment. We have to do it knowing that we may not get the reaction or answer we are looking for, and we have to do it through fear.

2 Corinthians 6:11-13 (NLT) reads:

> "Oh, dear Corinthian friends! We have spoken honestly with you, and our hearts are open to you. There is no lack of love on our part, but you have withheld your love from us. I am asking you to respond as if you were my own children. Open your hearts to us!"

I realize Paul is talking to them about not receiving his love, but I'm trying to show you how we can with hold our hearts because of fear and worry towards those who love us or towards those who may have hurt us.

Open your heart to those who have hurt you. That doesn't mean that someone who abused you or hurt you in an unsafe way is allowed to just hurt and hurt you, and you just open your heart with no caution (some people need to be removed temporarily and some permanently). It doesn't mean that you can't set boundaries but what it does mean is that you forgive and you listen, hearing the truth.

Maybe it's God you can't open up to because it feels like He doesn't seem to be near when you need Him. Maybe because of oppression, you shutter when you hear the Word of God, and your oppression comes from hurt. Either way, the truth is that it has caused a stubborn heart that needs to soften to flesh again. It can cause us to be lazy in our hope and internal journey.

Proverbs 18:9 (NLT) says, "A lazy person is as bad as someone who destroys things."

We can become lazy and complacent, and in turn, we become lazy in our relationship with God. That causes the destruction of faith, knowledge, and hope.

Laziness with God can destroy relationships, work environments, and our calling. Just like lazy people who litter, destroying the earth, so our laziness can taint our walk with the Lord, which in turn trickles down to everything else in life.

God doesn't want you just getting by with hopeless prayers and bound hearts. He doesn't want you watching sermons with an attitude of "yeah, right" because of your wounds. He wants you free of anything that comes against you.

Can you imagine if Jesus had placed all the hatred He received upon him? He was wanted dead from the moment He was born.

People mocked Him and turned their backs on Him, yet He still washed the feet of the man who would betray Him.

If Jesus held all of that in and didn't forgive or let it go, we wouldn't have the same Bible we do today. It would defeat the purpose of what we believe, which means when you don't forgive or lay it down, it defeats the purpose of His death.

Ephesians 1:17-20 (NIV) says,

> "I keep asking that the God of our Lord Jesus Christ, the glorious Father, may give you the Spirit of wisdom and revelation, so that you may know him better. I pray that the EYES OF YOUR HEART MAY BE ENLIGHTENED in order that you may know the HOPE to which he has called you, the riches of his glorious inheritance in his holy people, and his incomparably great power for us who believe. That power is the same as the mighty strength."

Your heart may be enlightened or opened, meaning, it's a spiritual awakening to be enlightened. When you're enlightened, you are free from what you once had or didn't know. And the hope in which He has called you? Well, hope represents a future for a calling in restoration. Restoration of your mind, heart, and kingdom, we are called to hope and to be a part of the restoration as His bride!

So, this isn't just for *YOU*, my friend. This is also for those who will know you and already do. They'll watch your *revision*, and make a *decision* about their own journey based on your new heart and your new actions. Your doubt will be removed, your ears will be opened.

To all those who doubt, I hear you and I understand. To all those who accept defeat, I say, rise to your feet.

Prayer

Heavenly Father,

Thank you for restoration and wisdom in its entirety. I pray that my heart is turned from a heart of stone to a heart of flesh, and I ask that you show me anything that resides in my heart that is not pleasing to you. I thank you for hope, love, and charity in abundance in my life. Help me to let down my guard and lay it all down just like you did for me. Remove any doubt that is holding me back.

In Jesus' name, Amen!

CHAPTER 10
Trust

Trust is the firm belief (similar to hope) in the reliability, truth, ability, or strength of someone or something. We even have trust in ourselves, but I'll admit there are things in this world that I don't trust myself with, and that's with anything white. Every time I buy a white pair of shoes or a white shirt, I immediately have regrets. I'm mad at those around me because I always think, "*Who let me get white?*" Like, it's someone else's fault that at almost forty years old, I'm too irresponsible for white.

I don't like roller coasters, I'm sorry if you do, but I think they're insane. I've been on them before, and all it does is confirm that I don't like them. The feeling of falling is so profound that I feel like I might die. I get it, it's dramatic, but hear me out. Who's building these roller coasters? Why do we trust these giant metal time bombs? You stand there for two hours, only to have it break down, and they break down often. However, they do get them up and running, but all I can think about is some high school kid going down with a wrench and a screwdriver, then boom, it runs for a few more turns. Don't even get me started on the rides at fairs, bungee jumping, and sky diving. The amount of trust we have in simply driving our cars that are constantly recalled for safety issues, is astounding.

We put our trust in so many things that make our day-to-day living run and even do dangerous things with mindless trust, yet we question God and perform a lack of trust when it comes to His love, blessings, mercy, grace, and promises.

Jeremiah 17:7-8 (NLT) says, "But blessed are those who trust in the Lord and have made the Lord their hope and confidence."

Psalm 91:4 (NIV) reads, "He will cover you with his feathers, and under his wings you will find refuge; his faithfulness will be your shield and rampart."

You have to trust someone to feel protected by them. You have to have faith and trust they'd cover you, and if you don't, then you won't find shelter with them, and you won't be dedicated to them.

I don't know why God is giving me a vision of, "*The Three Little Pigs*" right now, but He's telling me He's the brick house. The third little pig was the one with trust, the one with wisdom and faith, and because of it, He had protection (like Noah). Thank goodness He did so that the other little pigs had somewhere to run too!

Matthew 7:24-27 (NLT) reads:

> "Anyone who listens to my teaching and follows it is wise, like a person who builds a house on solid rock. Though the rain comes in torrents and the floodwaters rise and winds beat against that house, it won't collapse because it is built on bedrock. But anyone who hears my teaching and doesn't obey it is foolish, like a person who builds a house on sand. When the rains and floods come and the winds beat against that house, it will collapse with a mighty crash."

I had to trust at that moment where God was taking me with the three little pigs. I'm thinking about how juvenile it sounds, and it literally seems silly, but it's actually not! The wolf is the enemy trying to blow you down and he succeeds with some people because they didn't build their house on rock.

Because of my relationship with the Lord, I can tell what's happening. A year ago, I would have been like, "*Oh, that's so weird. The three little pigs just popped into my head.*" Now I'm like, "*Wow, the three little pigs, that's interesting; where are we going with it, God?*" Then, the child-like concept of the three little pigs led me to remember the Scripture about not building a house on sand. You need to place your life on a solid foundation.

I'm fully aware that not everyone's brain works like mine. The point is that God will speak to you in the way He made you, which is another reason to know yourself. No matter how He speaks to you, it's the trust you must have in what He's saying. It's child-like faith.

Psalm 28:7 (NLT) says, "The Lord is my strength and shield. I trust him with all my heart, He helps me, and my heart is filled with joy. I burst out in songs of thanksgiving."

What if, "Trusting Him with all your heart" meant trusting the breath in your lungs? Or healthy children, a job, a home. What if "He helps me" wasn't about this big thing that Jesus can do for us? What if it was just taking delight in everything he already helps us with? What if we took delight in just waking up in the morning?

Isaiah 26:3 (NLT) reads, "You will keep in perfect peace all who trust in you, all whose thoughts are fixed on you!"

I think we can place this big expectation on God and always need Him to do this great big profound thing in our lives, and we overlook what's right in front of us. We overlook everything He's doing, and we don't see the smallness as helping, but if we just started there in the simplicity of the everyday help, I believe that some of us would begin to trust a little more. Some of us would begin to regain a trust that is lost, and we would begin to build endurance with God.

2 Corinthians 5:7 (NLT) says, "For we live by believing and not by seeing."

Walking by faith and not by sight is something that they made a whole movie about, it's called, "Bird Box" and it's a Netflix original starring, Sandra Bullock. I'm just joking, it's not a movie about walking by faith, per se, but it is how we view walking by faith and not by sight. In the movie they have to walk around with a blind fold on trying to avoid evil. We think God has this blindfold on us, keeping us in the dark, and while I agree with you, it feels that way sometimes. God is saying, "*I gave you the gift of sight, I did not blind fold you, so what I'm actually saying to you, is to follow me even when you don't understand.*"

I know you feel as though He's glued the blindfold to your eyes, keeping you in the dark, but God is not the problem. Self-reflect and look at the plank in your own eye before blaming God. Find that missing puzzle piece because if you're not doing your part, which is walking out your faith, then He may do the one thing that, in my opinion, is the hardest task as a Christian, and that is to wait. Especially in this day, in the business of life and instant gratification, waiting is one thing we do *NOT* like to do. And yes, even when we walk out our faith he gives us seasons of waiting. I'm speaking about Him waiting for you to commit to growing.

We may ask, "What do you mean, be still and know? I just want to know!"

Can you imagine being Abraham and Isaac and the trust it must have taken to know without a doubt that God would come through? Do you think Abraham completely understood why God would lead him to almost sacrifice his son? (Genesis 22:1-19)

I mean, let's just break this down for a moment. God calls on Abraham to take his only son (love the significance of Abraham's only son compared to John 3:16) and sacrifice him as a burnt offering in the land of Moriah. Then, He tells him to do it on one of the mountains that He will show him.

So, as if the sacrifice of your only son isn't enough misunderstood trust, now he can't even know the exact mountain, God's going to reveal that later and Abraham has to trust that God will reveal the mountain. (Genesis 22:2 NLT)

So, Abraham gets up the next morning and prepares for the journey that would take three days. Again, more trust in my opinion, because that's a far place to go, and they didn't have a greyhound bus. They had a donkey and some sandals.

Abraham places the wood for the burnt offering on Isaacs's shoulders (we see a correlation here with the sacrifice carrying his own wood just like Jesus did). Then Isaac was like, "Dad, I don't mean to be a pain, I see you're deep in thought, and I know you told me to stop asking if we are there yet, but we have all this stuff for a burnt offering and no sheep."

I think Isaac was getting a little suspicious, if I do say so myself. But Abraham assured him that God would provide a sacrifice. He trusted that God knew what He was doing.

They arrived and started to build an altar, and before you know it, Isaac was tied up like a rotisserie chicken and placed on a pile of wood. I assume that wasn't cozy. Setting aside my absurd joke, when I read this story, I actually read it with so much peace and quiet as though it was so tense that neither one was speaking, but I can only imagine it wasn't that way.

This child that he was gifted and waited a long time for was about to be taken away. His son, whom he loved so much, was about to leave forever and the tears that had to be streaming from Abraham's face were probably gigantic. I can't comprehend the fear that Isaac felt while he was being tied up and placed on wood or the fear that Jesus had while being nailed to the cross.

Then an angel of the Lord stopped him from taking Isaac, and a Ram was provided in his place. I bet Isaac was like, "Dad, I know what you named me, but this wasn't funny, I am not the one who laughs right now!"

Abraham went on to be blessed even more because he trusted God, and God didn't bring him into his calling when he was Abram meaning "high father" He called him to do this after He had renamed him, Abraham, meaning "Father of a multitude."

A new name means a new promise in a new identity that you earned with growth and maturity, and I promise you, you are not given what you are not ready for, and even if you think you aren't ready, God knows when you're ready.

Sarai means "My princess," and after her maturity, she was then renamed by God to Sarah, which means "Mother of Nations." I noticed something beautiful about Sarah's renaming along with Abraham's. They both matured into the same calling, and they both became a "Parent of many". Talk about becoming one with your husband!

Being saved doesn't mean that you are always suffering or that God wants you in this perpetual state of sadness and trials. I used to feel this way because I was so oppressed. I didn't understand that joy and peace were for me to have and have abundantly. Yes, following Jesus isn't easy, and sometimes it looks easier on the other side of the fence. But there isn't eternity on that side.

People always say, "God never gives you more than you can handle" based on 1 Corinthians 10:13. However, I can assure you that you are given more than you can handle. You don't think that God calling Abraham to sacrifice his only son is more than he can handle? I really hope that Christians aren't saying to parents who have lost children, "God doesn't give you more than you can handle".

It says, He won't allow it with out providing a way out, He provided the ram.

God is saying don't worry about what you will eat, don't worry about what you will wear because if you trust in me, then I will provide it for you. So, when you read a book about becoming a new person, and it has suggestions of things you can do to walk that out, don't look at it as work. This isn't homework, this is your life!

I had to trust in a silent retreat that I was being propelled into by God and trust that it would be the unraveling that I needed. I had to trust I was beginning to heal. I had to trust He was for me. I had to trust that I was loved and worthy of it. I had to trust in my calling even if I *FAILED* forward getting there.

The point of this book is the simplicity behind God's design. I'm not saying God is simple but rather the ease of accessing who we are at any time. If you know who you are in any storm or in any season, then you can withstand a broken marriage, financial burdens, teenagers, and toddlers, all of it, and even things that seem like they can't be repaired.

I don't know what it's like to have cancer, and I won't say, "I can only imagine what its like," because I don't even think I could do that. I bet you can't even put into words the way you feel when they tell you the news.

But I have watched a wonderful, beautiful woman cast her worries to God and then when she showed up to her doctor's appointment, she was told that they could no longer find the cancer, and we praised God! This was her second time beating cancer.

A short time later, we would find out that she had cancer again, but this time it was in her lungs, and she had never smoked a day in her life. She was in her eighties and decided that since she was given just a few short months to live, she would ride out the last days as comfortable and happy as she could with her family. She rested in the peace of knowing that she would soon see her heavenly father, and she was ready.

We didn't like that she wasn't going to fight, but we accepted it. What else can you do? She was a woman of God who read her Bible and loved the church. She was always so happy and appreciated life. She wasn't innocent and got a little spicy in her old age, especially towards her husband, but after sixty-five years of marriage, I can only assume we become a little spicy here and there.

It's hard to see someone smiling one minute and in extreme pain the next. It's hard to line up and say your goodbyes to someone who you believe should live as long as you, I mean, why wouldn't she? She was a believer, and I thought she would always be here even though the math didn't make sense because she was fifty years older than me.

Why didn't God heal her again? Why did cancer come back if she trusted Him so much the first time? Can I tell you something? That peace she had, leaving and knowing that it was time to let go, was also trust.

My grandmother trusted that she would see her heavenly father and was never angry with God or her situation. Trust can be hard, but it can be as simple as trusting God's timing and His plan. He didn't give her cancer, but He did give her peace.

Proverbs 3:5 (ESV) says, "Trust in the Lord with all your heart, and do not lean on your own understanding."

We were all blessed to know the heart of our family, and not everyone gets to do that. We don't get to understand everything, and it's hard. When we tell a screaming toddler no, and they throw a tantrum, it's hard. They don't understand what's happening, and their emotions are out of control because they can't regulate them yet. Sometimes we can't either. When God says wait, it can make you emotional.

Who we are is something we have been gifted with. It's something we *CAN* understand if we are willing, and once we dive into it and realize He actually does have who we are accessible to us, then comes simplicity, and all other things will line up. So, knowing who we are will strengthen and put ease in our relationship with Him as He works through us, teaching us to rely on Him.

These assessments are not the "end all, tell all" of who you are, it's foundational. You get to work hand in hand with God to customize, talk out, listen and strengthen who you are called to be. The core of who you are is in the assessments, and that's why we can't change other people no matter how hard we try, and it's why we are not happy being anything other than ourselves.

So, which one are you, Sarai or Sarah?

Prayer

Heavenly Father,

I praise you for today and give you all the glory for every day and every moment. I admit that I struggle with trust and with things I do not understand. Help me to rely on you, help me to know your voice, and feel the Holy Spirit near me. Let who I am, grow and flourish, bearing good fruit. Let the maturity of my mind, will, and emotions change me for your glory. Let the trust I have in you be greater than anything in this world.

In Jesus' name, Amen

CHAPTER 11
Heaven On Earth

When we think of Heaven on earth, we think of euphoria or something that doesn't exist. However, we are called to bring Heaven to earth by releasing the kingdom of Heaven on this very earth.

Psalms 24:7 (TPT) reads,

> "So wake up, you living gateways! Lift up your heads, your doorways of eternity! Welcome the King of Glory, for he is about to come through you."

You get to be a living gateway! Writing this book is releasing Heaven on earth. Don't panic, you don't have to go build a homeless shelter to bring Heaven to earth unless you were called to do it, of course. It can be simple.

For instance, God spoke to me and talked to me about my sass. I was naturally offended and awakened at the same time. I grew up in a house where you just defended yourself with insults and sarcasm, so obviously, I would be mouthy and sassy to survive. Don't all siblings speak to each other that way? A lot of people outside of my family circle don't know me that way, which is good, however, we tend to hurt those closest to us.

The problem is that the sass wasn't just a comeback to a sister or a brother, it was disrespect to a parent, and it's being over the top to your kids, it's also a mean comment to a spouse.

I know I've already spoken about this a little, but it's important to know that being a strong woman doesn't entail sass that causes us to be rude or hurt others. We buy the tee shirts that say, "Strong and sassy" and we even put them on our little girls.

I told God that sass was just who I was, and He replied, "No, it's not!" He said, "I made you witty, I made you funny, and I made you bold, but I did not make you rude." This is something that I have to work on because I have been "sassy" for a long time. Sometimes my sassiness hinders me because I just stay quiet, knowing I have something sassy to say, so I say nothing during conversations with people I don't know. My sassiness isn't a rude comment to the person but rather a sassy joke or sarcasm that is better kept to me.

I'm also not talking about cute sassiness like playing around and joking with your husband or a comment to your friend that has pizzazz and lifts them up in a positive light.

If I'm checking out at the grocery store and the clerk is unfriendly and snarky, my immediate reaction is to stare at her with eyes of laser beams that say, *"I'm clearly a Karen right now, and if you don't be nice to me then I'll say something sassy."* That leaves me wanting to say, "Having a bad day?" Not the "Are you having a bad day? May I pray for you?" No, it's more like, "Your bad day is annoying me, and I deserve nice all of the time because I work in customer service, so I should know."

Thankfully, I don't act on it and I can remind myself that is not bringing Heaven to earth. You hear all the time when people say, "Don't be rude to rude people because you never know the news they just received or if they are having a bad day", and it's true.

Not long ago, I had a mother and daughter come in for blow out styles at the salon and the daughter was agitated because we asked for her information. She felt her name was all that was needed and was annoyed at our corporate salon questions. My fist thought was, "*Great, this ladies going to be fun.*" Her mother was quiet and seemed distant.

I ended up getting the mother in my chair, and after asking her how her day was going and what she was getting her hair styled for she replied, with a lump in her throat, "It's my husband's funeral today."

JIMINY CRICKETS! What if I had been rude to her? What if I added to her stress instead of taking some of it away?

Obviously, you don't let people completely mistreat you, Jesus said when someone slaps you across the cheek, you should give them the other cheek. However, I only have two cheeks (Your butt cheeks don't count), so I don't have to give you more cheeks than I have, and I will defend myself when necessary. However, we can be kind, sympathetic, and compassionate.

There have been times when I have been nice to people who were rude, and it brought a smile to their face, almost like they didn't even realize they were wearing their unhappiness on their face, or it's as if they needed that moment to snap out of the bad mood. Haven't you ever had someone make you laugh when you were being grumpy?

Christians are already not liked by many. Don't you think that by being little hellions instead of Heaven, we are harming ourselves rather than helping? Let me just put that in the form of a shorter statement; ***being a hellion instead of Heaven, will harm, not help.***

When I was pregnant with my daughter, I prayed for her to be bold but not rude, kind but not weak. My daughter sees the world through a lens of sunshine, rainbows, and sparkles. I always think to myself that I should have named her Joy because that's exactly what she is. I recently asked her what her favorite color was, and she said, "White with a unicorn, sprinkles, and cream." Those sound a lot like fancy pancakes or a cupcake, so I know for a fact, she's my kid.

In her mind, every outing is an opportunity to socialize, no matter the age, color, gender, clothing, or hair. You could be bald with three strands of hair left, and she will tell that complete stranger, "I love your hair!" With the utmost love and kindness, she means every word she says because she is naturally an encourager. This is also bringing Heaven to earth.

Hebrews 13:1-3 (TPT) reads:

> "No matter what, make room in your heart to love every believer. And show hospitality to strangers, for they may be angels from God showing up as your guests. Identify with those who are in prison as though you were there suffering with them, and those who are mistreated as if you could feel their pain."

Ok, so what if you don't want to tell bald men that you like their hair? You have other ample opportunities to bring Heaven to earth. Identify with those in prison? That makes being nice to a cashier sound a lot easier, doesn't it?

You are being used by God, and it should look like your normal daily Christian life, and you can do it through work, school, friends, and yes, even at the grocery store. It's crying with a friend, flying to Africa on a mission trip, writing a book, raising your kids, inviting someone to church, or serving in a soup kitchen. It's bringing the neighbor flowers. *Bringing Heaven to earth is just life with light.*

First, we have to remember we cannot do anything without God, and we have to submit to his authority. God is the authority. John 5:30 (NIV) says, "By myself I can do nothing, I judge only as I hear, and my judgment is just, for I seek not to please myself but him who sent me."

The Bible speaks of all different kinds of authority; for instance, parents have authority. Ephesians 6:1 (TPT) reads, "Children, if you want to be wise, listen to your parents and do what they tell you, and the Lord will help you."

Jesus was given authority, Matthew 28:18-20 (TPT) says:

> "Then Jesus came close to them and said, All authority of the universe has been given to me. Now wherever you go, make disciples of all nations, baptizing them in the name of the Father, the Son, and the Holy Spirit. And teach them to faithfully follow all that I have commanded you. And never forget that I am with you every day, even to the completion of this age."

We have the authority to approach God, Hebrews 4:16 (TPT) says:

> "So now we draw near freely and boldly to where grace is enthroned, to receive mercy's kiss and discover the grace we urgently need to strengthen us in our time of weakness."

Jesus was sleeping in the boat while a storm gathered and scared His disciples (Mark 4:35-40). In my opinion, Jesus was able to sleep because He had men with Him who possessed the authority to stop the very storm they awoke Jesus to cease. When they woke Him up with fear, He basically said, "Seriously, you bunch of chickens, why haven't you trusted and learned yet." Then He proceeds to calm the storm by telling the storm to "zip it" with His authority.

While Matthew 28:18 may be better suited for my chapter on spiritual warfare, I want you to see that ALL authority is given to us through union with Jesus Christ. With that union we are to go out as his gateway and us the authority that has been given to us to defeat the enemy and restore earth.

Forget superwoman, Jesus is your super power! Plus, you don't have to get dressed up in a tiny outfit and a cape while picking your wedgies. You get to be super from anywhere at any time, just sipping some coffee on the couch in your sweat pants. That's way cooler than superwoman!

You are seated with authority. Ephesians 1:19 (TPT) reads:

> "I pray that you will continually experience the immeasurable greatness of God's power made available to you through faith. Then YOUR LIVES WILL BE AN ADVERTISEMENT of this immense power as it works through you! This is the mighty power."

Always remember its God's authority and that while we would love to believe that certain rules don't apply to us, but they do as long as it doesn't go against God's authority. We have to pay our taxes, pay our bills, go to work, etc.

Romans 13:1-2 (TPT) says,

> "Every person must submit to and support the authorities over him. For there can be no authority

in the universe except by God's appointment, which means that every authority that exists has been instituted by God. So to resist authority is to resist the divine order of God, which results in severe consequences."

Bringing Heaven to earth is abiding in Him, John 15:4 (TPT) says:

"So you must remain in life-union with me, for I remain in life union with you. For as a branch severed from the vine will not bear fruit, so your life will be fruitless unless you live your life intimately joined to mine."

I've often met women I knew were Christians because it was radiating off of them, or they spoke in a way that would lead me to believe they were saved. I often ask God to make it known to me in areas where I'm not displaying His love. Sometimes it's just a nudge to say to someone, "I'll pray for you." That alone seems simple, but sometimes it's scary in the way that you often get rejected as a believer. I've told people that I would pray for them, and they've laughed at me. It didn't feel good, but it's better than having a crown of thorns crammed in my skull like Jesus.

I'm a hairstylist, and there are two golden rules when talking to your clients. No religion and no politics. So, naturally, we talk about religion and politics. However, as soon as I do, I regret some of the conversations that I get into.

I have to remember there is a time and a place for certain conversations and that talking about certain beliefs doesn't necessarily bring Heaven to earth. I'll never deny my beliefs, my God, or political stances, but I have to remember that all eyes and ears are open, and I may be having a conversation that could lead a listener in the wrong direction.

You're probably thinking, who cares if nosey Nellie hears my political views? My point is this; would those around you know you're a Christian or just an opinionated conservative? What are you known for? Up your God game, my friend, I have to always check myself, especially in a work environment where I'm the only believer walking in alignment with God.

Authority is the power or right to give orders, make decisions and enforce obedience. Obedience is compliance with that order. Obedience is submission. Don't give in to the things of your past now that you know better. Continue to grow into who he created you to be. 1 Peter 1:14 (ESV) reads: "As obedient children, do not be conformed to the passions of your former ignorance."

Sometimes it's not the act itself but the word. When we hear authority or obedience, we hear dictator because we aren't thinking of God. We are thinking of someone ruling over us. A dictator is someone who takes total power *BY FORCE*, like Hitler or an abusive spouse. Authority is a position *GIVEN* unless you are God because He *IS* authority.

A police officer is given authority to keep certain laws in place for citizens' safety, hence, public safety. Your boss is given authority to give you deadlines and even fire you if need be. I'm trying to implement that sometimes authority is looked at in a negative light, especially if we have wounds from authority. If a husband manipulated and ruled over a wife, telling her when and how to cut her hair, what she can wear, eat, and what size she should be, then that is just plain abusive. And that is an abuse of authority and more of a dictator.

We get our basic morals from a law, do not steal, murder, envy, disobey our parents, etc., and even unbelievers don't realize that their basic morals and values come from the authority that was given to Moses, who wrote commandments that we follow today.

So, again let's make sure we are looking at authority not as a tainted word but as a word given as a gift from God for many reasons. If you are a believer and God is authority, and Jesus was given that authority, then it's something you should value.

Luke 6:46 (ESV) says, "Why do you call me 'Lord, Lord' and not do what I tell you?"

This Scripture right here makes me want to smack one of my kids upside the head. Here is an example, they fall off of a chair that you told them five times not to stand on because they would fall and get hurt, but now they're crying for you, and all you have to say is, "Didn't I tell you not to climb on that?" Yet, you still console them because they're your child. This must be how God feels.

Obedience is love, and I always tell my kids when they gripe about not being able to do what the other kids are allowed to do that, *if I didn't love them, I wouldn't care what they did.*

For instance, bedtime is important to me, and when it comes to kids getting enough sleep, research shows that it's extremely important. Even my teenagers have a bedtime, and phones do not go into the room during bedtime. Of course, they push back about how they are the only ones amongst their friends with bedtime during school. However, they're also happy when they can actually get up in the morning and function.

I'm not saying that if you don't give your child a bedtime, you don't love them. Rules are different in every home. My point is that a child left to do whatever they want whenever they want with no regard for authority can become disobedient, and that's not love because children need guidance. How do you teach them not to burn themselves or keep them from wandering on the road? You set a rule and teach them that it's not safe, and if they try it, then there is a consequence. That is love.

John 14:23 (ESV) reads, "Jesus answered him, "If anyone loves me, he will keep my word, and my Father will love him, and we will come to him and make our home with him."

Keeping Jesus' Word and obeying Him, is love.

The reason we sometimes seek other things and look elsewhere is that we don't have a relationship with God, and in turn, we don't know His will for our lives.

We work out and acknowledge that eating healthy is a life style change. I mean, we literally say, "It's not a quick fix, but a life style change". We need to acknowledge that spending time with God is a life style change.

Sometimes we count it all joy and sometimes even with that joy we need discipline to engage.

Your life style should look different as a believer and you don't owe anyone an explanation (unless you are guiding them, or the Holy Spirit prompts you too) on why you attended a retreat that contains a 48 hour vow of silence. You don't owe anyone an explanation on why you wake up and pray, or why you pray over your food, or why you don't go to the club anymore.

It's who you are, it's what you believe, it's who you follow, and it's about the One who lives with in you. I'm not suggesting that when you're at work, and praying over your food and someone ask, "Why do you do that?" that you reply with, "BECAUSE!" No, you respond with love.

I'm speaking about a person who decides to say it in a condescending tone, "Oh, so you pray over your food, that's weird." Yes, you still respond with love but you don't owe them an explanation that they don't truly want anyway. Just keep responding in love and planting a seed.

Hebrews 13:20-21(NLT) reads:

> "Now may the God of peace who brought up from the dead our Lord Jesus, the great Shepherd of the sheep, and ratified an eternal covenant with his blood may he equip you with all you need for doing HIS WILL. May he produce in you, through the power of Jesus Christ, every good thing that is pleasing to him. All glory to him forever and ever. Amen!"

He will equip you when you spend time with Him.

Jeremiah 29:11-13 (NLT) reads:

> "For I know the plans I have for you," says the Lord, "They are plans for good and not for disaster, to give you a future and a hope. In those days when you pray, I will listen. If you look for me WHOLEHEARTEDLY, you will find me."

This Scripture says for "I" know the plans. The "I" isn't for you, its God speaking to you as in He knows the plans. We've heard about all different kinds of wills, like; ethical will, good will, free will, and a stubborn will. He has a will when it comes to plans for you, and it's a will that you don't know unless He reveals it to you.

We like to walk around saying that God will give us all the desires of our hearts. Well, I hate to be the bad news Betty, but we have to dive into that a little.

Psalms 37:4-5 (TPT) reads:

"Find your delight and true pleasure in Yahweh, and
he will give you what you desire the most. Give God
the right to direct your life, and as you trust him
along the way, you'll find he pulled it off perfectly."

Delight, in the biblical sense, actually means to mold or to bend.
So, you should be pliable, obedient, and willing in order to have
desires. When you give God the right to direct your life with a pliable heart that He can mold into His will, you are actually letting
God change your heart, and then His desires become your desires.

Obviously, we desire a home to live in or a new pair of shoes, or
a vacation. God is a loving God who will grant the things we desire,
but what we are talking about here is a change of heart that will
propel you into His will and desires.

2 Peter 3:9 (NLT) says:

"The Lord isn't really being slow about his promise
as some people think. No, he is being patient for
your sake. He does not want anyone to be destroyed,
but wants everyone to repent."

He's literally being patient while he waits for our hearts to
repent and change. For our will to be His, to walk out our call-
ings and bring Heaven to earth with our love and kindness, and
the Lord's patience gives people time to be saved. Plus, while He's
waiting, He is asking us to help Him be a vessel leading people to
our Lord Jesus Christ by using our Strengths, Spiritual Gifts, Core
Values, and Five-Fold Ministry.

You are not called to figure out everything in your life right
now, but you better start working on a better version if you haven't
already. I assume you picked up this book because, like me, you were

confused. Then it's your job to let God take you from confused to confirmed, and that doesn't happen by putting this in the corner and not doing the work.

You are not called to be some perfect person with a perfect house and perfect kids and a perfect body. You are called to walk out who you are in Christ, and it's your job to use the tools in this book to figure it out and become the healthiest version of you so that you can ignite the beautiful things in your life that you were given like, Joy that overflows, peace that subdues, patience that endures, kindness in action, a life full of goodness, faith that prevails, gentleness of heart and strength of spirit. (Galatians 5:22-23)

I know that I don't know you personally or what you are going through, but God does, and He wrote a book (the Bible) so awesome that it can pertain to anyone and everyone, no matter the circumstances.

In the Bible, He called a hated tax collector and murderer to rise up in his name and bring Heaven to earth. He can also call an oppressed girl who struggled with sexual immorality, relationship failures, a teen pregnancy, doubt, and unclean spirits to rise up in his name and write books to bring Heaven to earth. But first, I had to lay it all down, and I had to reflect, listen, seek and find, wait and do all the vulnerable feelings I didn't want to do or feel.

I fought it, and I fought hard like a bull rider who just keeps getting back on the bull, I wasn't giving up on my own ways because, gosh darn it all, I wasn't wrong, everyone else was, and I was causing harm that didn't need to be there. This doesn't mean that the people in your life didn't do wrong. This means that you are focusing on what *YOU* brought to the table.

We long to know who we are, and we have all these tee shirts out here saying, "Not all who wander are lost." Yes, you are Becky, so stop it and sit down, you're literally wandering and lost! You're searching and seeking for something that comes from a father, your heavenly father.

Listen, I know that for some, we struggle longer than others, my theme song for life thus far would be Britney Spears. "Oops! I Did It Again." Not so much the song itself, but I pretty much nailed the name of it. The first year I got saved, I had plenty of times that I would come to church hung over from the night before and wondered if they wouldn't mind turning down the lights and music.

Thankfully, I was able to set alcohol aside and slowly progress. But, don't be me. Don't take eleven years of lukewarm salvation and mind-wracking to live out your life.

Growing into your salvation takes time because we need time to learn God's Word but staying stagnant in our growth isn't God's version of growth.

So, lay it down because you are co-crucified, do not resurrect your pain. He died for you, so when you don't heal, it's like kicking dirt in your own face because you were co-crucified with Him (Galatians 2:20-21). God gave me what I believe is a revelation of why the serpent was cursed in the way he was.

Genesis 2:7 (NLT) reads:

> "Then the Lord God formed the man from the DUST of the GROUND. He breathed the breath of life into the man's nostrils, and the man became a living person."

But watch this....
Genesis 3:14 (NLT) says:

> "Then the Lord said to the serpent, because you have done this, you are cursed more than all animals,

domestic and wild. You will CRAWL ON YOUR
BELLY, groveling in the DUST as long as you live."

So, Adam was formed from dust on the ground, and the enemy
was cursed to crawl on his belly. Well, in order to crawl, you'd have
to be low on the ground. The enemy is then told, he will grovel
in the dust.

The devil is literally cursed to a lifetime of humility in the very
dust Adam was made of, and he's angry about it.

So, get out of the dirt! You don't need to be there with him,
stand up, bring Heaven to earth and remember these are just a few
of the ways to bring Heaven to earth. Go and dive into the Word to
seek out how Jesus wants you to bring Heaven down and sprinkle
it around.

Start with you, spread it out in your home and to family, then
friends and strangers, and even your calling. Just being strong and
courageous is bringing Heaven to earth! You're on a journey, and
once you exercise being a slice of Heaven, it will click, and you'll be
spreading it all over.

Know who you are in Christ by doing the work provided or
attending a Kallah Unveiling Intensive. Take the assessments from
the websites provided and study them so the enemy can't trick you.

1. Get rid of any oppression or unclean spirits.
2. Once you know who you are, walk in it, and then walk in your
   calling once it is revealed.
3. Spend authentic time with God creating a relationship with Him.
4. Know Jesus and allow God's will to become yours.
5. Find your tribe and find your community, remember it takes a
   village and even if you have church hurt, find a new tribe, and
   just keep going!

6. Bless others (compliments, serving, etc.)
7. Share God's Word.
8. Obey Him
9. Invest in yourself, time with God can be in many different ways, but the important part is that you discover how you need to invest into the best you that you can be. Maybe it's a women's retreat or a Bible study every week or setting time aside to go on a walk by yourself, it doesn't matter. It's for you and God.
10. Watch how you speak to others and yourself.
11. Stop trying to have earthly perfection and give yourself grace. If you need a class on finances, take it. If you need a class on how to raise your kids, take it. You can't be everything for everyone. God knows that, and He just wants you to be who He created you to be so that you can share your awesome self with the world shining your light, praising Him in any storm, and bringing Heaven to earth through His Word that touches others.

1 John 4:7 (ESV) says, "Beloved, let us love one another, for love is from God, and whoever loves has been born of God and knows God."

You are His beloved, go walk as though you believe it!

Getting Ready

There is a song by Maverick City Music and UPPERROOM called "Getting Ready" and it's so beautiful. If you haven't already heard that song I recommend delighting in it. Have you ever thought about what it means to prepare yourself for Jesus?

You pick a groom, a day, and a dress. The excitement is intertwined with anxiety and stress but the vision is beautiful. You hope every aspect goes accordingly. You've carefully sought out each color for the flowers and you can no longer stare at Pinterest because you've looked for weeks to find the perfect hair style, and the perfect shoes.

You've given so much time and thought into preparing yourself and getting ready for such a beautiful day. What else in life have you prepared for? College, children, or maybe a dead line at work? We have all had to prepare for something in life. But nothing is more important then the preparation of becoming His bride.

Revelation 19:7 (TPT) says,

"Let us be glad and rejoice, and let us give honor to him. For the time has come for the wedding feast of the Lamb, and his bride has prepared herself."

In Scripture we see bridegroom and we see bride. Bridegroom is a representation of a man who was just married or about to be married. It's used to represent Jesus and the church is the bride of Christ. Saying yes to Jesus was your first step in preparing yourself as the bride.

We take so much time out of our lives to prep and we often neglect our relationship with God. I want you to accept that knowing who you are in Christ and taking the steps to heal, grow, and discover who you are in Him is preparing yourself.

When you get a job aren't you trained in that specific job? To compete in a marathon you have to prepare and train to do that as well. Why a person would want to train to run a marathon is beyond me be but I do admire the person who has the talent to do so.

Discovering who you are is self care and it releases you to heal and excel in the body of Christ. You will unveil yourself, when you start to prepare yourself.

An unveiling is a presentation or revealing of something that was once unknown or hidden. Yes, we are unveiled as new believers but we have to grow into our salvation, ever learning and laying ourselves down to become new. Let the old melt away and transition yourself into a new beginning.

Becoming saved and then doing nothing is like getting married and then never seeing him again. You might call and touch base to see how they're doing but you weren't quit ready to commit all the way.

If you've ever prepared for something in life then you owe it to yourself to prepare for this. You deserve to know who you are in Christ and to be blessed with the knowledge that God created you with intention!

List your Gifts of the Spirit:

1. _____

2. _____

3. _____

4. _____

5. _____

List your top two Five-Fold Ministry:

1. _____

2. _____

List your Core Values:

1. _____

2. _____

3. _____

4. _____

5. _____

6. _____

7. _____

List your Strengths:

1. _____

2. _____

3. _____

4. _____

5. _____

This is the foundation of who you are in Christ. HE LOVES YOU!

Giftstest.com, Fivefoldministry.com, Gallup.com, and Kallahculture.com

Lightning Source UK Ltd.
Milton Keynes UK
UKHW022007010223
416340UK00023B/279